Pic taken in Middlesbrough with George at the Pig and Whistle pub

Pic with Robbo at the Riverside during a book signing session

Pic from Rome with the White Feather

Pic with Sir Bruce taken in Denmark

Pic with Chris Rea in a Newcastle hotel

C000142356

Bernie's About

Bernie Slaven's Unedited Interviews

Bernie's About

Bernie Slaven's Unedited Interviews

The Road to Eindhoven

A unique and at times hilarious record of the adventures of Middlesbrough Football Club as seen through the eyes of Alastair Brownlee and Bernie Slaven.

Never in their 25 years plus experience of covering or playing for the Boro did either ever dare to dream about reaching a European final.

But Boro did in just their second season in Europe – a remarkable achievement.

This book takes you on a journey from South Wales to the Netherlands. A journey which took two years to complete and one which lasted over 40,000 miles through 14 countries.   £15.00

The Class of '86

In 1986 Middlesbrough Football Club came within 37 minutes of going out of existence.

The Class of '86 is the story of how the club was reborn and went from liquidation to a glorious promotion, a time when fans rediscovered their pride in their football club.

Without the class of '86, what followed – six cup finals, including one in Europe, and Premiership status for the 10th successive season at the start of the 2007-08 campaign, would not have been achieved.

This is the remarkable story of the Class of '86 in the words and pictures of 13 players, their manager Bruce Rioch, his assistant Colin Todd and the fans.   £10.99

Bernie Slaven Legend?

Long before the Riverside Revolution, Bernie Slaven was God to a generation of Boro supporters. As a prolific striker, he was a goal-greedy, burger-eating teetotaller who couldn't seem to get his head around the offside rule. Boro fans loved him.

Reborn as a media pundit, he is the outspoken, irreverent, backside-showing Voice of the Boro - and he still hasn't grasped the offside rule. *Most* Boro fans love him.   £12.00

Voice of the Boro

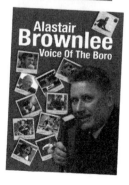

1967 was the year that Ally started supporting his home town club, 15 years later he swapped the terraces for the press box. Ally has commentated on more than a thousand Boro games and continues to this day..

This book gives you an insight into life as a commentator (a biased one at that).   £12.00

All titles are available to purchase in all good bookshops and online at www.linthorpepublishing.co.uk

'SUCCESS IS NOT WHEN
PEOPLE WANT YOUR
AUTOGRAPH------
THAT'S FAME AND GOES AS
QUICKLY AS IT CAME.

SUCCESS IS LIKE A MONUMENT
THAT SURVIVES LONG AFTER
YOU ARE GONE.'

I DEDICATE THIS BOOK
TO THE LATE GREAT
WILLIE MADDREN

Willie was the man who gave me my big break back in 1984.

Despite finishing Scotland's top goal scorer, there was limited interest if any, for my services.

It was local a journalist's idea that I sent letters to the Scottish premier league clubs and the first and second division in England. It was the last thing I wanted to do but I felt obliged when Andrew Gold turned up at my family home with a pile of letters and stamped addressed envelopes. He politely asked me to sign them and sent them off.

After a couple of weeks the replies started to come in. Only one Scottish club replied; Heart of Midlothian. Unfortunately, it said, they could not offer me a contract as they had taken up all their allocation of professionals.

Clubs such as Chelsea, Arsenal, Watford, Crystal Palace, to name but a few, wrote back in similar fashion.

The first positive reply I received was from Middlesbrough FC.

I was invited for a trial against Grimsby Town.

My first social meeting with Willie was at the Billingham Arms at a sports night. He offered to buy me a drink. When I ordered a Coke he looked suspicious, as if to say 'who are you trying to kid?'

After the Grimsby game which ended up 0-0, I returned to Glasgow. I had been invited down for a month's trial, but I had a part time job and wasn't going to put that at risk, I simply could not afford to.

I remember phoning Willie's number to explain that I wouldn't be coming down for a month when, suddenly, an answer machine message came on with Willie's voice on it.

I had never heard an answer machine message before.

I hesitantly said 'thank you for inviting me for trial, but I won't be coming.'

A couple of days later, chief scout Barry Geldart made contact and invited me for one more trial game, the opposition was Bradford at Ayresome Park.

The game ended 4-2; I created 2 and scored 2.

The following day I signed a 2 year contract with a 2 year option and trebled my salary.

Without Willie's foresight, knowledge and determination to give me the opportunity I might have still been in Glasgow doing the parks or on the dole.

I hope I made Willie proud with what I achieved at Middlesbrough.

My biggest regret was not being able to interview Willie due to his poor health.

Therefore I dedicate this book to the late great Willie Maddren.

A top professional and a true gentleman.

ACKNOWLEDGEMENTS

First of all I would like to thank the players, managers and celebrities, for giving up their time free of charge and allowing myself the opportunity to interview them over the years.

I would also like to thank Ntl and Boro TV for creating 'Bernie's About' which was a weekly segment on cable television.

A big thank you must go to a close friend of mine Graeme Banderia, for his time effort and creativity with the cover design, his biggest quality of course is being a Boro fan.

Thanks to the Evening Gazette, Highland Studios and the players themselves for providing the pictures.

A massive thank you to Clarissia for typing, formatting and translating my scribble into this readable book form.

And also thanks to you the public for buying it, hope you enjoy your read.

INTRODUCTION

The Bernie's About idea came when I worked for Boro TV between 1998 and 2002.

Over those years I met some of the greatest players ever to wear the red shirt of Middlesbrough as well as some of the high profile managers.

The job involved travelling up and down the country accompanied by a camera man. I met players at hotels; in the comfort of their own homes; training grounds; even on boats. Over a period of time I interviewed over 200 players, managers and personalities - and thoroughly enjoyed doing every one of them.

Some were clever, outspoken, outrageous, opinionated, quiet, eccentric, charming, smug and even arrogant, but everyone was an individual. And to their credit none of them asked for a fee. They gave up their free time and answered my questions openly and honestly and made me most welcome.

It was an honour and a privilege interviewing World Cup winners, European Cup winners, people who have been successful in their profession.

I hope these unedited interviews in written version give you, the reader, an insight into what their characters were really like.

Contents

'I had played for England, I had played for teams that had played all over Europe, my qualifications were not in question, maybe it was just me, my personality.'

Jack on why he didn't get the England job.

Take 1
Jack Charlton

Jack was born in Ashington, Northumberland on May 8th 1935. As a player he notched up a record 629 league games for Leeds United between 1953 and 1973.

On his retirement, Jack expressed an interest in league management and was offered the job at Middlesbrough and accepted the post on May 7th 1973.

I met up with Jack at his home in the outskirts of Newcastle.

Jack was charming, funny, and ruthless; he was the only manager that had the happy medium. By that I mean he could mix with the lads for a laugh and a drink and a sing song but during training sessions or a match day he was the boss whose toes no-one dare stand on.

I recall a scene which I had never witnessed before during a training session; it was during Italia 1990 World Cup. It was an 11 verses 11 game and up front for the first team 11 was John Aldridge and Tony Cascarino. From the start of the practice game Jack was on Cascarino's case. "Cas get your touch right, Cas head the bloody ball, Cas hold the dam ball up," Jack snapped and shouted. "Cas if you don't get yourself sorted you're out."

5 minutes later Cas was out and Nial Quinn replaced him. Not just for training but for the forthcoming World Cup game against Holland. In all my career I have never witnessed a manager dropping a 1st team regular because of a poor training session. Rightly or wrongly Jack proved who was boss.

Big Jack is one of the loveliest guys I have ever met, he's a straight talker with no airs and graces; what you see is what you get.

Before the interview, big Jack demanded I bought him fish and chips. It's not everyday you sit down to eat fish and chips with a World Cup winner. I felt honoured.

JACK

Listen Bernie, before we start, do you still talk to the dog on the phone?

BERNIE

I told you not to mention that. Of course I do.

JACK

Well I was a little bit perturbed at you showing your arse on television by the way, my players don't do that.

BERNIE

I apologise Jack.

You started your playing career at Leeds Utd. Were you a bit disappointed that it wasn't Newcastle? You must have been a Newcastle fan as a youngster?

JACK

No, nobody wanted to play for Newcastle at that time and our mother wouldn't allow us to play for Newcastle. At that time they wanted our kid (Bobby) to go and they wanted me to go for the trials and things like that. What they used to do then was play you in the Newcastle (ends) and then you never got heard of again. By then you were resigned with them so no-one could have you, and that was apparently the way it worked in those days. It's changed since then of course, but eh, I got an offer to go to Leeds for trial and eh, I decided to go there.

BERNIE

You spent 22 years at Elland Road, how did you last so long ?

JACK

Well you take the first few years out. I went at 15 and became a ground staff boy as they called them in those days. Not an apprentice a ground staff boy; you did your work on the ground, you worked in the dressing rooms and you cleaned boots and the toilets and you did all the jobs.

BERNIE

You had me doing that with Ireland.

JACK

Now and again.

And then I had a year at 17 when I signed professional. Then I had a year I played in the 1st team, one game, then the reserves in the Yorkshire league. Then you had a 2 year period when everyone had to go in the army. So I didn't really pick up playing football professionally until I came out of the army at the age of 20. Then I went straight into the 1st team at Leeds and I was in there for the rest of the time until I was 38.

BERNIE

You started off as a full back, is that right?

JACK

I went and had a trial as a full back yeah and eh then I had never played centre back. I played at full back, probably wasn't good enough to be a centre back, cause full backs were always the bad players in those days.

When you decided to pick a team, what they did was the best players play up front, the next ones midfield and the other ones at centre back. The last ones to get picked were the full backs. So I started as a full back then very quickly they moved me to centre back at Leeds and that's where I played the rest of my career.

BERNIE

What were your greatest achievements at Leeds?

JACK

Oh I don't know.

Just being there for 22 years and being with Don Revie 10 or 11 years, when we didn't win as much as we should have done but we competed so much in every other competition that, eh we were always involved in the league; we were always involved in the cups; always involved in European competitions, played any number of games between 65 and 70 games a year, mainly at the end of a season when things became frantic, because the season finished, then before the cup finals your games had to be out the way, then the final was at the beginning of May and it really was very difficult to focus.

When all you're doing is playing important game, important game, important game right the way through till the end of the season, when you're playing 2 and 3 games a week, we didn't win as much as we should.

The year we sort of opted out of the other competitions, or got out of the competitions, we went on to win the championship no problem.

BERNIE

Leeds had the reputation of being a dirty side, would you agree with that?

JACK

No, you can't say a dirty side. We had a couple of players that could well look after themselves and caused us a bit of aggravation, sometimes I mean I've yelled at my own players for some of the things they did, we had a bit of a reputation when we first came into the division. 1965 when we got promoted and we got to the cup final against Liverpool, we had a bit of a reputation then. Things started to change over the next few years, then people suddenly realised that Leeds Utd weren't a dirty side, they could look after themselves but they were also a very very good side. In fact, one of the best sides, people said, that this country produced for a long long time.

BERNIE

Is that up until you met Celtic?

JACK

Yeah, well Celtic beat us in the semi final of the European Cup. That's the only thing I didn't win at Leeds. I never won a European Cup winners medal, we got beaten by Celtic and beaten by Hamburg the German side.

BERNIE

In 1966 you were a member of the England team that won the World Cup, how did you do it, was there a secret?

JACK

No we just had some good players. I mean, people look in respect and say, I mean, Sir Alf Ramsey said that England would win the World Cup before the World Cup took place, everyone had a little smile and ...

BERNIE

Was he psychic?

JACK

Yes, but when you've got people like Bobby Charlton and Bobby Moore and we had Jimmy Greaves, one of the top players in the business, we had a lot of good players in the England squad at the time and it was no surprise when we won it really.

BERNIE

Do you think England will ever win it again?

JACK

Not the way we are going at the moment.

With as many foreign players, and they seem to be taking the limelight rather than the English players, who are pushed into the background now.

And our national team were never prepared properly for anything since that last World Cup.

It's difficult to put your finger on why, but every other country, the national team is the pinnacle and the top, in England you always get the impression that the league here is more important than anything else, the national side takes second role to that. It's only in the last 3 or 4 years that they have actually allowed England players to cancel the game on the Saturday, so they have got time to prepare 10 days before an international match instead of 3 days that they usually got.

BERNIE

What kind of player were you? I've heard so many stories I want to hear it from the horses mouth?

JACK

I was awkward, a good competitor, I didn't like to lose and eh people have said uncompromising, I suppose they're right I don't know, I couldn't play the way other people played.

I was good at stopping other people playing, which people laugh at when you say it but it's true. I mean, I was good at stopping other people playing, I was a good keeper of the ball. I was a good tackler.

I learned all the things in the North East of England before I went away and eh how to do things in the right way, don't mess around in your 18 yard box, get rid of it, get it out, be effective.

I always believe that centre backs should be one touch players, you don't want to be pulling balls down and doing clever things on the edge of your eighteen yard box. If you make one mistake you've lost the game.

I look at so many players now in the English football league when they sign a centre back, they say yeah he's great on the ball.

That would frighten me to death. I don't like players who play centre back who are like that. I think you've got to be effective, I think in the years I played with Norman Hunter we were both effective.

BERNIE

You left Leeds Utd after making over 600 league appearances, you ended up joining Middlesbrough in the summer of 73. How did that come about?

JACK

Er, Doc Phillips was the England team doctor at that time.

I had seen Middlesbrough play once before and I thought they looked quite a good team and Stan Anderson was there at the time and they had some good players.

I felt they just needed a couple more players to make things happen. When I went, it was a team who had not quite done enough to get into the premier division or the first division as it was called then.

Stan left and he had left me some good players.

I mean, I found Graeme Souness playing left back or left half, I mean he was never quick enough to play in those positions, so we moved him into centre midfield.

I had Alan Foggin who was a winger, but I played Alan Foggin in midfield because he was a great runner. And at that time the whole of the game was being played by teams who played strict offside, they would push up. So what you had to do was play the ball behind them and have somebody running from the midfield who wasn't offside. Eh I tried to institute that at Middlesbrough when I went.

The big problem with it was David Mills and John Hickton because both of them were runners for the ball. John wanted to get to the far post and compete for headers. David Mills was quick at turning but he was turning and running offside, so I introduced Alan Foggin into midfield alongside Graeme Souness. I got Bobby Murdoch, who was a great passer of the ball, I also got David Armstrong who was a great passer of the ball, and we let Foggy run, and when teams were pushing out to play offside, he would run from midfield, he would play in behind them. The moment it got there we all backed it up and it worked a dream.

BERNIE

You had some very talented players during your time at Boro, Maddren, Souness,

Murdoch. How did you manage to get Murdoch on a free? Jock Stein must have been mad?

JACK

I don't know, I sat next to Jock at a football league dinner in London. And eh, we just sat there next to each other at a football writers' dinner and he was asking did I need any help.

I had just taken the Middlesbrough job, I said "well I'm looking for a right sided midfield player and 1 or 2 other players." And he said "well I will give you Bobby Murdoch." So I said "you'll give me him?"

He said "yes I will give you Bobby Murdoch," I said "how much?" He said "no it's ok, just look after Bobby."

BERNIE

You didn't get a bung did you Jack?

JACK

No, no.

We looked after Bobby.

Bobby came. He was only 28 at the time, carried a bit of weight, he worked very hard and became a great player for Middlesbrough for 4 years. He was one of the best passers of the ball you ever saw, you would swear blind that when he was running the ball would quicken up to catch him if he was going too fast, or it would slow down if he was going too quick. Fantastic passer of the ball.

BERNIE

When you joined Boro you said you would last 4 years and you were true to your word. Why 4 years?

JACK

Well I knew a man called Jim Bullack. He was a big labour man and he used to say to me never stay in a job for longer than 4 years, because people get to anticipate you and they know exactly what you're thinking and likely to do, so 4 years is enough. You can't then start to introduce change 'cause people won't accept it. The only way to introduce change is to find another club .

So I said 4 years fine, and I did my 4 years. I was tempted to stay another year because we had a few quid at Middlesbrough at that time.

BERNIE

Why did you not spend the money?

JACK

I don't know.

We had money and I could have bought and stayed another year and maybe we would have had a chance of winning something, but I decided that the 4 years was right and that any manager coming in behind me, it wouldn't have been fair for me to spend the money that season, simply because he would want to spend it his way.

Whoever took my job took my place because it was my decision to leave, and I left. And I once said to somebody doing an interview like this, probably the biggest mistake I made in management was not staying at Middlesbrough another year and I think that was probably right

BERNIE

After leaving Middlesbrough you spent 5 years at Sheffield Wed before returning to Middlesbrough as caretaker manager. Why caretaker?

JACK

Well I done my 5 years at Sheffield Wed, and I was having a bit of time off, I've never gone from one club to another club to be manager. I've always had a little break in-between.

And I was having my little break after Sheffield when Mike McCullagh phoned me up and Malcolm Allison had left and they were in a bit of trouble in the second division. He asked if I would come back and see them through the rest of the year.

Considering Mike was a friend of mine - he joined the Middlesbrough board on the same day that I became manager - I said "ok Mike but I'm only staying until I've kept you in." And we did, we stayed quite comfortably in the division .

Then I left. Mike wanted me to stay but I didn't want to. I said "I'm leaving now". We played I think I'm not sure who it was, we got a draw somewhere and we were safe in the league and I said to Mike "that's me" and I left.

BERNIE

On leaving the caretaking post you had a brief spell at Newcastle before being appointed Republic of Ireland manager. How did that come about?

JACK

Well, I never wanted the job at Newcastle. Jackie Millburn talked me into it, he was on the phone to me all the time.

They couldn't find anybody to take the job funnily enough. Arthur Cox had just left they had got promotion, Kevin Keegan had left, Terry McDermott was out of contract and looked like he would be leaving and he did, and they asked me to keep them in the first division for a year, just do a year and stay in the first division, which I agreed with them. I said "ok I will do the job for you."

We kept them in the first division and I got trapped in the job and couldn't find a way out.

I had to go to the tribunal with Chris Waddle at the end of the season because he was going to Tottenham. Then when I should have left I didn't and it finished up, the first excuse I got was.

We played Sheffield Utd. I think Gazza played in his first game that day, a friendly match pre season and er the way I remember it, we went out for the game and during the game a section of the crowd started to yell at me and started shouting Charlton out, and all this business, I couldn't understand what it was for, cause it was a pre season friendly, we hadn't even kicked a ball in the league yet. It was apparently because I had being going to sign Eric Gates from Ipswich, and he wanted too much and they wanted too much and I cancelled the deal on the Friday and on the Saturday Lawrie Mcmenemy signed him for Sunderland, so really he had become a maccum rather than a Newcastle player and the crowd didn't like that.

But it was my decision, but it gave me an excuse to do what I wanted to do. I had done my year, what I said I would do and I wanted out, but I couldn't get out. It all finished up pretty nasty. I really didn't want it to finish that way.

BERNIE

Leaving Newcastle you went to the republic, how did that come about?

JACK

Well I didn't go straight away. After I finished at Newcastle I was doing nothing, I got offered jobs in different places then I was sat at home just before Christmas and I got a phone call asking if I would be interested in the Irish job. I said I would then I went away to Spain for 2 or 3 weeks.

When I got back I got another phone call to say are you still interested, I said "yes" then I got another phone call to say I'd got the job, and that's when it all began.

I just went away with the Irish, had a good look, I didn't know the first thing about the Irish and their football team or anything, I don't think anybody else did either. We settled down to a way of playing, got the lads going a little bit, started to improve the team. The people in Ireland liked what I did and that's all that's really important.

BERNIE

Did you receive any stick from your mates being English and joining the republic?

JACK

No, not at all.

I remember walking through Dublin on the day I got the job and everyone in the streets just kept stopping me, shaking my hand and saying well done, hope you enjoy it, hope it works out for you and all this business. I've always been well received by the people. I don't know why but the Irish took a liking to me, in fact I was probably one of the most popular Englishmen in Scotland funnily enough. For whatever reason they always love me when I go to Scotland, I don't know what it is.

BERNIE

They certainly like you better than that Jimmy Hill. A compliment.

JACK

Not exactly.

BERNIE

As republic boss you took Ireland to Euro 88 and 2 World Cup finals in Italy and America. What was your greatest moment?

JACK

Oh we had good moments.

When you see the team improving and you're beating people, I mean we beat Brazil, we beat Brazil in Dublin, we beat any team in Europe that's of any consequence over the period that I was there.

We went away to the World Cup, we did quite well in the first one in Italy, we went to America and beat the Italians, we went down to Orlando and couldn't handle the heat, it was just one of those things.

It finished not as well as we would have liked it to finish cause I felt we had a good enough team to do well in America, but we didn't make it and I will always to this day blame the heat, cause some of our players couldn't handle it at all. It was enjoyable with the Irish.

To pick out a game and say that one gave you the most pleasure. The ones you get the most pleasure from are the ones you win that qualify you for the competition. And strangely enough we never qualified in Dublin, we always qualified away from home for various competitions.

BERNIE

Why was that?

JACK

I've no idea.

BERNIE

Every time you called up a player to the national squad people questioned their background, did that annoy you?

JACK

It did and it still does to this day.

The qualification for Ireland is exactly the same as for England, Northern Ireland, Scotland and Wales. You can go back as far as your grandmother to qualify to play for that country, if you can prove her place of origin to be in that country. This happened with the 2 people I signed: John Aldridge and Ray Houghton.

Now Ray Houghton was born in Glasgow and he's a Glaswegian but his father was born in Donegal so he's well qualified to play for the Republic. John Aldridge on the other hand, we had a hell of a job finding where the church was, that his grandmother was married and buried in, when we found it he could get a passport and qualify. People made a big deal of this but I mean Ireland was only a small country, we didn't have any number of players playing, we had to get players from where we could. If they qualified we had to get them.

I couldn't pick a team out of the league in Ireland that would qualify for anything. If you want to compete with the best in the World Cup, you have to get the best players you can, which is what I did .

We had a good nucleus of solid Irish people, Kevin Moran, Mick Mcarthy, Paul McGrath, Tony Galvin. I mean the ones that had been questioned were actually before me like Mark Lawrenson was questionable, but Mark was great for us up until he got injured.

I did get annoyed and I'm answering the question in a long way this time because it did annoy me. The complaints come from people who couldn't beat us, like the English couldn't beat us and they didn't like it

BERNIE

You left the Republic job in 94/95 season. Was the timing right?

JACK

I was always going to retire, like I mentioned earlier Jimmy Bullack also used to say to me; as soon as you turn 50 retire if you can afford to.

BERNIE

You could certainly afford it Jack

JACK

Not when I was 50 I couldn't. If you can afford to retire when you're 50 do so, cause you then go into the last 10 or so years of your life when you're fit enough and able enough to do the things that you want to do, not the things you've had to do.

I never made it at 50 but I made it at 60, so I resigned, virtually. I told them on my 60th birthday that I would be leaving at the end of the qualification.

If we qualified I would stay over the summer. If we didn't qualify I would leave the day we didn't, and they knew that from the day I turned 60 .

We had a party in Bolton, everybody came over. I was always going to retire at 60 and I did.

BERNIE

Why have you never managed England. Would you like to have managed England?

JACK

Everybody that played for their country would like to one day manage their country.

I felt I was overlooked by the English at a time when I was probably the most. Strangely enough I was a staff coach with the FA from a very early age, I had always been a FA lad, I had always done my badges all the coaching certificates and all the things that were necessary.

I had played for England, I had played for teams that had played all over Europe, my qualifications were not in question. Maybe it was just me, my personality, maybe they didn't want someone like me in that sort of situation. I mean, Brian Clough never got the job either.

I remember 2 or 3 members of the committee that were picking the team phoned me and asked me to apply, so I did, and I never got a reply to the letter but they had people there who had nowhere near my qualifications, or played at the levels that I had played at, or looked at the levels that I had looked at. I mean I worked for ITV for years, I was at every game that was important anywhere in Europe. I was at every World Cup, I knew international football inside out but I never got an invitation to manage the England team.

I would have liked to have been asked but I never was.

BERNIE

Well Jack, thanks very much for talking to me. I love that jumper you're wearing by the way.

JACK

(With a massive grin) Ok Bernie, let's go fishing.

HONOURS

JACK CHARLTON

PLAYING CAREER HISTORY

1952-1973   Leeds United
1965-1970   England.

MANAGING CAREER HISTORY

1973-1977   Middlesbrough
1977-1983   Sheffield Wed
1984   Middlesbrough (caretaker)
1984-1985   Newcastle United
1986-1994   Republic of Ireland.

PLAYING HONOURS (winners)

England
1966 World Cup

Leeds
1964   Division 2 Champions
1968   League Cup
1968   Inter Cities Fairs Cup
1969   Football League Champions
1972   FA Cup

MANAGERIAL HONOURS (winners)
Sheffield Wed
1980 Division 3 Promotion
Middlesbrough
1974   Manager of The Year
1973-1974   Football League 2nd division

CAPS   35 Full caps for England.

‘ *It certainly wasn't luck and I don't mean that conceitedly, 'cause you can't get lucky 40 times a year. You can get lucky 5 times, but not 40.* **’**

Referring to his 40 goals
a season.

Take 2

Brian Clough

Cloughie was born in Grove hill Middlesbrough on 21st March 1935. He became a full time professional at his home town club in May 1952 and made his league debut in September 1955, against Barnsley. In total, Cloughie made 222 appearances for Boro scoring a phenomenal 204 goals.

I travelled to Nottingham to meet Cloughie.

At the time, Brian's house was being renovated; that was old big head's excuse anyway, so we met up with him at his big mates home - a guy called Colin Lawrence - to do the interview. When Brian arrived he shook everyone's hands then nestled down in his seat. As we had a pre chat he turned to my mate who weighs 28 stone and asked "are you from the boro then?" Next question was what school did my mate go to, then boy you must have ate some school dinners. Everyone in the room burst out laughing.

Cloughie was everything I expected, controversial, opinionated, outspoken, charming. Before the chat I asked, "would you like me to go through the questions with you?" "Carry on young man" was his well-documented catch phrase.

Looking at the past and present goalscorers over the years at Middlesbrough Cloughie, without doubt, is the greatest to wear the red shirt of his home town club.

He retired from football management in 1993 and sadly passed away on the 20th September 2004.

I was honoured and privileged to meet one of the games most charismatic and successful figures.

BERNIE.

You were born and bred in Middlesbrough. What was it like growing up in the Boro ?

CLOUGHIE.

Well I was very happy Bernie, extremely happy, err I fell into football because I was thick academically, as you've already established this morning.

And err I was extremely happy born and bred in Valley Road, near the park. I was obsessed with sport, even when I was a little child, neglected school obviously like a lot of us did in those days, and I was very, very happy.

We used to live next door to the steelworks football club and they had a cricket pitch also and I was a fanatical cricket fan. It was cricket obviously during the summer, when we got a summer in Middlesbrough, we didn't get a lot of sun in Middlesbrough.

It makes me laugh when all these foreign players come up to Middlesbrough, you know and after about 6 months the wives say "oh we can't stand the weather," and I turn to my wife Barbara and I say, "you know I never saw one palm tree in Middlesbrough while I lived there for 20 odd years, I never saw a bloody coconut until I went abroad." And she says she can't stand the weather. What the hell does she think it is in Middlesbrough, bloody sunshine like Florida?

Anyway Claireville, Steelworks Club, and Albert Park, that was my 3. When I eventually signed for Middlesbrough I used to walk through Albert Park but inevitably I was late so I used to run through and walk back afterwards.

BERNIE

Who were your boyhood heroes?

CLOUGHIE

Well it was the whole of the Middlesbrough side; they were full of heroes you know, Middlesbrough Football Club considering we won nowt.

We had the Wilf Mannions, the Mickey Fentons; I followed Mickey Fenton into the side, George Camsell, Alex McCray, who was one of your lot.

BERNIE

I'm Irish.

CLOUGHIE

You're Irish are you, you don't sound it. There was Jimmy Gordon, who worked with me for many years afterwards, Harry Bell who played wing half they kept floating out all these, so it wasn't just one particular hero we had a lot, we had a bloke called Blenkinsopp who was rumoured to have only played when he'd had a couple of pints before the match. It was all rumours, but he certainly had one after the match I know that. Dickie Robinson he played, he got in with the England side eventually and they were good players and they were regarded as a very exciting side but as I say we won nowt.

BERNIE

You played football for Billingham Synthiona and Great Broughton. Who was it that spotted you?

CLOUGHIE

Well I went to Great Broughton which is a farm, it's a village just outside Middlesbrough, and errrr I went through my brothers, I played with the 4 of my brothers at Great Broughton when I was 15 or 16, I played for Billingham Synthonia because I worked at the ICI.

BERNIE

I played for them last year.

CLOUGHIE

You look older, and I played for Billingham Synthonia, one of the first clubs I got a few bob from. In those days you used to play 3 nights at the end of the season, and I got a few bob from Billingham for expenses, more than I was getting working for the ICI, 'cause I was a messenger boy at the ICI and I played for South bank and got a few bob from Southbank, but Great Broughton was the initial thing, and of course my brother was several years older than me, our Dez was older than me. Billy was older than me and I was the 4th in line, and I got in the side when I was about 16 I think.

BERNIE

Who was it that actually spotted you?

CLOUGHIE

To get up there it was just family connections, it was just about you're ready you can come up. We used to go up on a potato lorry in the back, Sanderson's had a firm.

BERNIE

I think I saw that last week.

CLOUGHIE

You would have done, it will be the same lorry as well, and he'd deliver his stuff into Middlesbrough and then he'd pick us up at lunch time and take us to Broughton, we'd go into a pub and play darts until it was two-o-clock, until they got the sheep off the field, cause there was bloody sheep on the pitch and they had to clear the sheep off the pitch before we could start and I enjoyed it.

The women who used to run it ran the post office at Great Broughton. They called her Nancy Goldsmith, gee that's a long time ago.

BERNIE

4 years after joining you made your first team debut against Barnsley. Do you remember anything about that?

CLOUGHIE.

I remember the guy I played against, Harry Hoff they called him, blondish going bald wing half, I remember playing there, I think we lost .

I remember the immortal words that Bob Dennison said to me as we were walking out of the tunnel, out of the dressing room to the tunnel, a real booster to me he said "Well it's up to you now," and he said that to me, a real booster, and there I was going out on my debut, and I'd had a pretty good time at Middlesbrough reserves, but I was still 4th choice and then eventually I wound my way through and got in against Barnsley and we lost, but err I stayed in the team and then went out again.

BERNIE.

People described you as a brave, confident, ruthless, centre forward. How would you describe yourself?

CLOUGHIE.

Well I was certainly brave because I was thick enough and young enough not to know about fear, only intelligent people know about fear. You know older people say to me all the young men that used to fly aeroplanes during the war, they weren't thick but they didn't know about fear, but once you know about fear you are frightened and err if you tend to think about your job, you get frightened on occasions, but err I wasn't frightened.

I used to take the centre halfs on as part and parcel of my job you know, despite the fact that they were kicking me for three quarters of the game, I used to take them on as equal, and err I had a knack.

I can't explain why I scored more goals than anybody else. I knew I liked scoring, and some of the criticism I got was from my mates at Ayresome Park.

They'd say "the only time you talk is during the match, and all you shout is pull it back so you can score," I said "well who's the best goal scorer in this team," "well you get your 40s like," I said "well I'm the best so you might as well give it to me."

Played with a lad called Ronnie Burbeck, fat little lad played outside left and he brought that up in a team talk, he said,"he's always shouting for the ball boss," he said "when he gets near the penalty area," I said "well I tell you what, the next time I shout and you ignore me go and put it in," I think he only got 4 goals a season.

BERNIE.

You spent 7 seasons at Ayresome Park. Did it frustrate you that you never actually played in the top flight.

CLOUGHIE.

Yes, it frustrated me personally 'cause I was in the goals and I was scoring enough goals for two teams to get promotion. I know there was a lot of goals in those days, more than there is now in modern day football, but when you're getting 40s as I was getting, I was getting, 38, 39, 40, 41.

BERNIE.

Was there a goalkeeper in those days?

CLOUGHIE.

Eye, there was goalkeepers.

I used to stick them through Sam Bartrams legs, he used to play for Charlton, but I was in the brackets of over 40 you see, to score all that many goals and not win something. It was ridiculous, there were sides getting promoted every season in the 2nd division, scoring half the goals we were scoring, but we couldn't keep a clean sheet to save our lives, and that stood me in good stead when I went into management, 'cause my first priority when I went into management was to keep a clean sheet, and I built on that .

I built every team I've ever managed on a clean sheet. I bought Shilton, he nearly bankrupt me. I bought him for £300,000, his wages were astronomical even in those days, and somebody said, "what have you bought Shilton for?", I said, "well he doesn't exactly score goals but he saves 15 a year and that's 15 points to me." And of course he did, he was an amazing goalkeeper, he did nowt for 89 minutes and even in the European cups, that we were winning in those days, he'd do nothing, nothing, nothing then somebody would let fly at him from 25 yards, and he'd get his fingers to it, and he'd walk off and he wouldn't be dirty or anything, but that one save would have saved us the match, incredible player.

Then I used to be obsessed with centre halfs because I used to work with a lad called Peter Taylor who was a player at Middlesbrough. Bob Dennison bought him from Coventry and I became friendly with Peter at Middlesbrough and err the relationship lasted right through our careers, until he went to Derby and I stayed and all that type of thing.

I was obsessed with centre halfs and goalkeepers and he was obsessed with goalkeepers 'cause he was one, so I formed my opinions in management when I first started. I'd get myself a goalkeeper, I'd get myself a centre half and then I'd get myself a centre forward to sneak a goal and if you look at my career that's what I did do, it sounds easy but it wasn't that easy.

BERNIE.

You scored 204 goals in 222 appearances. How did you do it? Was it anticipation, was it greed?

CLOUGHIE.

It certainly wasn't luck, and I don't mean that conceitedly, because you can't get lucky 40 times a year, you can get lucky 5 but not 40. Somebody once said to me when I was manager of Derby County, they said "oh lucky to win the league" when we beat Leeds. You can't get lucky over a season to win the league, you can get lucky over one match or two matches, but when you play 40 odd games you can't get lucky every match and err I got annoyed.

When I came to Derby of course I was still young enough to play football and I was playing a testimonial for a lad called Edwin Holliday who used to play outside left for Middlesbrough, and he was at Peterborough, and I went to play

DELIVERY NOTE

1

DATE

Delivered to

By

To TALIA
Best WISHES

RECEIVED BY

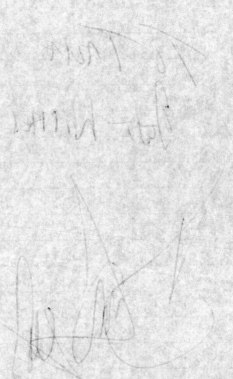

in a testimonial and I was manager of Derby and I picked meself, well a good start when you're the manager, so I picked meself and we won 1-0, and I scored the goal. It bobbled in the far corner, we had a welsh man playing with us called Alan Durban who finished up managing Sunderland actually. After the match he said "Is that how you got all your goals?" I said "yeh about 90% of them," I said "bobbling in luckily, you know off my backside, off my chin off me eyes, if I could put them in with me ear I would," and I said "I used to catch them in the middle on occasion and they used to go in," I said "It was 90% of 40, every season that bobble in." And that shut him up for ever more like. I said "I used to have the occasional screamer, and you scored all your goals in the box," I said "Well that's where the penalty area is and that's where the posts are," I said "The only thing that doesn't move on the football pitch is the posts."

BERNIE.

Some of your players and fellow professionals describe you as big headed and arrogant.

CLOUGHIE.

I was certainly arrogant and I was certainly conceited to the strength of my own ability, but it wasn't a bit of arrogance, it was just, that when you know what you can do, I suppose that is arrogance. I suppose 'cause it came after a couple of years, you've only got to score 40 goals a couple of seasons running and you're bound to know after that, that you can score goals, so if that's arrogance, yes I was arrogant.

I had done my national service and I didn't get married early. I didn't get married until I was 24 which was late in those days. You know you used to get married when you were doing your national service, the first one you knocked off where ever you were stationed you married.

BERNIE. You had experience of that more than I did.

CLOUGHIE

I waited and then I was lucky, I fell on my feet or my wife fell on her feet actually.

We met in Rea's café along from Ayersome Park, where I used to spend some of the best hours of my life, drinking milkshakes. I met Chris Rea the singer, I don't know whether you're interested here but Chris Rea is a good singer and I met his family there cause they used to run the Rea's café, and I'm certain I've clipped young Chris many a time, because you used to clip anybody that got in the way. It was a way of life in Middlesbrough, anybody smaller than you got a clip. Cause I got my fair share, that's why I've got big ears now, and err I met Barbara there and we went on from there.

BERNIE.

While captain of Middlesbrough, 9 of your so called team mates signed a petition for the captaincy to be taken away from you. Did you feel betrayed?

CLOUGHIE.

Oh yes certainly did, I certainly did.

Bryan Phillips was the centre half in those days. We bought him somewhere and he said "I think I can do the captaincy as well as you" and I said "If you can then get it done." Like you know, and we were all on no money those days, and I wasn't too happy with the way things were going, I felt we could be winning matches that we weren't winning, of course I then made a stand and left Middlesbrough.

I didn't really want to leave them you know, I was born and bred in Middlesbrough, once you're born in Middlesbrough you don't want to leave you know, and especially as I had gone up through the ranks .

Anyway, I set my stall out, I'm leaving this club because there's something the matter with it, and of course eventually when I did leave, and I went to Sunderland I was regarded as a traitor in many areas of Middlesbrough.

I still lived in Middlesbrough for a period of time, then I moved to Sunderland when I got married, or after I got married, but it wasn't "Eye up Cloughie how are you, you're at Sunderland." It was terrible, it was only up the road Sunderland but they never forgave me. But of course when I was at Sunderland, it all came out about Middlesbrough that some of the players were selling matches, and I twigged it. A couple of them went to jail actually, I wish they would have all gone.

BERNIE.

Have you got one abiding memory of Ayresome Park, one that sticks in your mind?

CLOUGHIE.

When all this trouble was on, we played Bristol I remember, 3 that match, we won and I stuck a hat-trick in. Len Shackleton came to me after the match cause he was working for a newspaper in those days, he'd finished playing, Len Shackleton, and he said, "Well I've seen some good hat-tricks but that's as good as I've seen," he said "I think we should have a row every week." and errr things like that, and of course I played for err, I played for err, the football league. I got me a couple of caps while playing for Middlesbrough, err you know there weren't tons of memories, but it was just a continuous roller coaster in the sense that I was just on it and I never got off it and being Middlesbrough born and bred you knew everybody.

Err I used to walk through the park as I've told you to go training or run and the keepers of the park, the gardeners, I used to say to them about October, when they used to change the beds of flowers, "Hey, when's your wallflowers coming." "We will let you know Cloughie when they come." As soon as they bedded out for the winter, cause wallflowers don't flower till, you know, March-ish, the first flowers out wall flowers, depending on the winter, and err I would be going through one morning and he would say "I've got your wallflowers." He used to have them in a wheelbarrow, he didn't charge me or nowt like that, there was no money changed hands, hell no money changed hands for 25 years in my life. You used to get on the buses for nowt, they used to let me on the buses when I got on a bit, not to your level but I got on a bit at Middlesbrough, and I used to get the occasional cake for nowt from Sparks, and I used to get my milkshakes and she gave me a Cornetto as I was going out the door once for nowt, and that was me getting on.

They're on bloody £30,000 quid a week now, but I used to get me wallflowers in the barrow and it was just that kind of place, simple as that.

I used to run up to the Palladium, go to the butchers shop and the chairman of the picture house at the Palladium building was the chairman of the football club. They called him Steve Gibson and he used to come down Valley Road in his great big bloody car, and me ma would either be cutting the privet, it was my turn to cut the privet when I got to 10, I started cutting the bloody privet, she'd either be sweeping the bloody paths or scrubbing the steps and Gibson used to go past and I'd say "Mr Gibson just passed." He used to give us the bloody royal wave, in this bloody big car and of course we didn't have a car. I never had a car until I was 25 or 6, and he used to come down on his way to the ground, he used to call in the buildings up there, he had the picture house and various shops and he was the chairman of the club.

BERNIE.

You earned 2 full England caps. Should it have been more?

CLOUGHIE.

I was disappointed with Walter Winterbottom, he was in charge those days, Walter Winterbottom, and I regarded him as an amateur, and he stayed in charge of England for a long, long time.

I got capped at Wembley against Sweden, we lost, the first time Sweden had beaten us at Wembley, and I got capped at Cardiff, against Wales obviously, and I had just scored 4 goals the previous week or fortnight, against the Welsh centre half, a lad called Mel Nurse. I stuck 4 past him and they were all expecting another 4 in the international, and I never got a bloody kick, and we drew 1-1.

I was rooming with Jimmy Greaves, and Jim had either just got married or was on his way to getting married, 'cause his misses was out there and it was pouring down, she was like a bloody drowned rat standing in the rain, cause we all used to stand in the bloody rain in those days, and if we could get our wives a ticket even for England it was brilliant just to get them in for nowt.

BERNIE.

On the subject of England, why have you never managed your country? I asked Jack Charlton the same question.

CLOUGHIE

Well I thought I had got it, I went down for an interview and Jack was on the short list actually. I think there was him, he went down, I went down and Lawrie MacMenemy, went down, there was 3 of us for interviews.

Once again this might sound conceited, but you know when you do a good interview, you know they used to say to me "How did you feel when you came off having scored 3 goals." You knew when you played well and when you didn't nobody knew better than you, you know, you know yourself when you've been good or bad or indifferent, and I had done a good interview at Lancaster gate, and I went back to the hotel where some friends were waiting for me and I said "Well if it goes on interviews I got the job," cause I doddled the interview.

Anyway, they finished up giving me the England youth side, and they didn't give Jack the job either and he was qualified to get it, they didn't give Lawrie it and he was qualified. They gave Ron Greenwood it and he wasn't even on the shortlist I don't think.

I think they had just settled for his type and his image. Ron Greenwood was a charming man like Walter Winterbottom, but they weren't our type of manager.

And the reason I give now, I still give to this day as I'm talking to you, I didn't get the job because, I think the football association suspected that I was going to take over the football association.

BERNIE.

You probably would have.

CLOUGHIE.

Absolutely, certainly. I would have closed half the offices down for a start. I'd have the team first on the aeroplane in the front seats not in the back, 'cause all the bloody FA wallers used to go and they used to have the big cigars, the gin and tonic and the smoked salmon and we were nowt.

Even before I started playing for Middlesbrough, me dad's favourite player was Wilf Mannion and Wilf played for England. They went to Scotland and Billy Liddle used to play for Liverpool. I think he broke Wilf's jaw, they didn't set it at the hospital and Wilf came back the next day, stood in the bloody corridor of the train, couldn't get a seat and with this broken jaw.

That's how they used to treat footballers, and Wilf was the best inside forward, well he was playing for England, he was a God here. And George Hardwick, they were Gods in Middlesbrough they were.

BERNIE

You signed for North East rivals Sunderland. Was that a difficult decision?

CLOUGHIE

It was a difficult decision, 'cause I never wanted to leave Middlesbrough obviously. I was born and bred in Middlesbrough and was part of the furniture. Errr, to go to Sunderland was kind of being a traitor to the Middlesbrough fans, and I was very, very happy at Middlesbrough. Simple as that.

I had been on holiday and I'd signed up for a cruise and I went with somebody else and the 4 of us went, I went with an older couple and we docked at Southampton coming back, and there was this guy waving to me and I was getting the suitcases off and looking to see if I had 2 bob, cause you had to give everybody 2 bob to carry your suitcases and he lowered me suitcases on this trolley and Barbara said, "I think he's waving to you." I said "No, no bugger knows me on a bloody cruise." I said "the only guy who got to know me, I was cheating at deck tennis." I was playing him every day, deck tennis and he says "You're overstepping the mark." Any way it was Alan Brown on the quayside waving. I went down, he said "I'm going to sign you for Sunderland." I said "Well I know nowt about it." And I didn't. He said "Well I'm signing you." And that was it. I thought about it all the way home in the car, in me pal's car, I said "Well I've kicked up enough stink at Middlesbrough wanting to get away." I wanted to go in the 1st division, which I did Sunderland I think were going into the 1st division and err I went and signed for them simple as that.

I enjoyed it there very much, people at Sunderland think I am a Sunderland man, which I wasn't. I'm a Yorkshire man a Middlesbrough lad, but I had a very, very happy time at Sunderland, they all took to me straight away. Me 2 sons were born in Sunderland, so that you know me 1st son, me 2nd son, my daughter was born in west Hartlepool, so they regard themselves as Northerners, and I was just happy at Sunderland simple as that.

And it showed, it actually came when I had finished playing through injury, they gave me a testimonial and I got 31,000 there for me testimonial, now that wasn't bad, there wasn't 5 clubs in the country that could get 31,000 for a league match never mind a testimonial.

BERNIE.

Goals continued at Roker Park 53 to your credit, then you suffered a serious knee injury which ended your career, what was the injury?

CLOUGHIE

I hit a goalkeeper it was an icy day, one of your lot was in charge Howley, Kevin Howley, he was in charge, and I used to know Kevin very well and we were walking round the pitch, and he said "What do you think." I said "Well its boxing day and the bloody crowds in, they were in at half past two." I said "You've got to put it on." So I influenced him really. So we put it on, it was an icy pitch and I got a ball played through from a lad called Jimmy McNab, he couldn't play football to save his life, and I chased it and I wasn't looking at the goalkeeper and I always used to keep my eye on him, and he came and hit me half way on me knees, I went over him and bust me curciate ligament and me medial ligament and a cartilage. Now they can do curciate ligaments, but in my day you couldn't do them and me bloody knee was wobbling about and never became stable. Now they drill the bone and put a knot at the other end, but they couldn't do it then and I finished playing on the Boxing Day simple as that.

BERNIE

So how did you cope you were only 27?

CLOUGHIE

Yeh well Mr Brown the surgeon, he set me left leg in plaster from the ankle up to the top of me leg, and he set it bent so the medial ligament could heal quickly, me leg was like that bent and I always had big quadriceps and everything so I spent another 3 months getting me legs straight.

I was training on me own which is a killer training on your own when your injured, and I was going back mornings and afternoons, Brownlee was a right hard master, err I used to go into the ground at 5 to 10 and he'd be standing in his office looking out the window and he used to come down at 10-o'clock, and he used to say "I'm waiting on the day I catch you coming in gone 10," and I always used to get in at 5 to 10 by the time I'd got down the bloody stairs, I'd be saying "What time we going training."

BERNIE

How did you cope with the injury?

CLOUGHIE

When I got injured at Sunderland George Hardwick was manager and he pulled me in and there was no barrier on wages and I was on £40 a week, when I went to Sunderland which was a fortune, and I got injured and I was in plaster and Hardwick called me in , he said " if you think your going to hang around here for a year injured earning £40 a week, you've got another thing coming" he said " you're in charge of the A team for tomorrow" and this started me off. That's where I met Colin Todd.

I met Colin Todd playing for the A team for Sunderland and eventually Rolls Royce went bankrupt in Derby, and the whole town went bloody bankrupt, you know it was like the ICI closing down in Middlesbrough the whole town, when they went bankrupt they cleared the building societies out of the money and there was big long ques, everybody was out and I went back to Sunderland and signed Toddy for 170,000 quid, which was an absolute million. I came back and the chairman nearly fainted, I said "I've done some good business today" he said " what have you done" I said " I've signed a lad called Colin Todd" " oh yes and who does he play for Brian" I said " he's playing for Derby tomorrow" "oh yes , what did he cost?" I said "170,000" he never spoke to me for a year.

BERNIE.

You started your managerial career at Hartlepool along with ex Boro goal keeper Peter Taylor as your number 2, was that a good place to learn your managerial role?

CLOUGHIE.

Well it was the only job I got offered erm I took the job the night I got me testimonial.

I took over Hartlepool that night as well. But what broke me heart was , you had a manager called Raich Carter who once again was an idle in football in general and Raich had played for England, I think he played for Derby, and he played for several clubs anyway, but he was in the Wilf Mannion bracket Raich Carter was and Wilf was in charge.

The journalists used to go down as I've already said on Tuesday and I got a lift down with one of them and went into see Raich and said "I'm finishing, I've been in charge of the Sunderland youth side for the last 6 months or whatever, any chance of me coming and starting at Middlesbrough in charge of the youths" he said "oh I will ask them". And he went to a board meeting, I went back the following week and he said " no they won't have you back" and I said "the board won't have me back" he said "yes the board" . I didn't quite believe him at the time, because I had not upset the board of directors or anything, I never seen them from one month to another .But Raich turned me down for me first job in football, and it set me back of course. I thought like all footballers you take your boots off one minute and you become a manager the next.

I wanted to be a manager, I knew I wanted to be a manager when I was 25 eh but Raich turned me down. I could have been sitting where you're sitting now, working for Middlesbrough if he'd have taken me on, you will never know.

BERNIE.

Leaving Hartlepool you steered 2nd division Derby County to promotion, then the 1st division title in 1972. Was that purely down to your managerial skills, or was it having quality players or a mixture?

CLOUGHIE.

Well we signed the players. Err the 1st signing I made one of the 1st signings, I signed Roy McFarland from Tranmere, then I signed Archie Gemmel from

Preston, then I got Juan Rodisson , he came from Birtley near Newcastle in between Sunderland and Newcastle.

We got a Kevin Hector who came from Bradford, we had a nucleus of a side there and I signed John O'Hare and Colin Todd from Sunderland err and Dave McKay from Tottenham, he was the best one cause he was 32 and I was managing a side 21 plus and I was only 30. Dave McKay was older than me and he was still playing.

BERNIE

You moved to Nottingham Forest, where you won the first division title in 1978, and won the European cup twice in 78 and 79 seasons. How did you do it, you weren't exactly loaded with cash?

CLOUGHIE

Well we got all the players as I've said I signed Kenny Burns one of the best signings ever. And err I was judging a sweet pea show at Nottingham sweet pea, I was judging the show. I said "I will meet you at the garden centre" where it was being judged, half way to Nottingham cause he was coming from Birmingham..

Well he turned up in a car if the coppers had seen him they would have arrested him just looking at the car, he had no tax disc, one side was all bashed in, I said "how about insurance" he said "what's that" "you've no insurance either" I said "get to the bloody ground, get out of my sight, I will sign you at the ground".

And players used to place an awful lot of trust in me. They used to sign blank forms and I'd say when all the staff come in on Monday I'll fill it all in, don't worry you will get exactly what I promised. And they always signed blank forms, did it for years. I was proud of it actually.

So we go to the ground sign theses forms, so I say to Burnsey " right I'm going back home, like you know it's my bloody day off" he said "well give us a couple of pounds of those peas, I'll take them home and give them to the wife and we will have them for lunch tomorrow". I said "they're bloody sweet peas". He said "what not the ones you eat" I said "no not the ones you eat". So that's how we signed Kenny Burns, that's how I signed him and he was a smashing lad, he comes to see me now.

He lives in Derby actually, and he was a good player ooh was he a good player. He gave me as much as anybody gave me, bloody hell he frightened everyone as well, he frightened the Spanish to such an extent.

I played against Barcelona in a European cup ,not the European cup we have mentioned, another competition their champions verse us and I beat Barcelona in it, and they went out to sort him out in Spain, oh they went at him during the match, and I'm shouting Burnsey kick the, the normal words kick the ball and ermm

There was 4 going at him and he was, whacking it and whacking it, and he turned round when he cleared and said to the Spanish, he couldn't speak English never mind Spanish Burnsey couldn't, he said " and you're the next if you come anywhere near me" and they soon got the message and they scarpered from him. And he used to give Shilton some stick he'd say to shilton "you're the best goalkeeper, they tell me you get more money than any body else at this club, do you know why you're the best goalkeeper" and Shilton used to say "no" like you know Shilton was very quiet like in the dressing room Kenny was the opposite. Kenny used to give me stick, never mind out else and he used to say "you're the best goal keeper cause they never get to you, I take all the bloody flack for you, me and Lloydy". There was Burnsey and Lloydy and if they ever got past the 2 of them without getting kicked Shilton used to come out and spread his bloody self, and you couldn't see the goal, so they used to miss the bloody target, by about a yard. Burnsey used to say "I take all your flack as a matter of fact I should get half you're wages.

BERNIE

Trophies followed in the 80's but you were relegated in 93, why did you retire after relegation?

CLOUGHIE

Well I didn't feel as if I had enough time in the game, but I certainly was considering retiring 18 months before I did, err I know that it sounds blasé now, but I'd been in management fairly young, you know I didn't play till I was 25 and then had a quick entry into management.

I went into management when I was 30, 31, and I was thrown in at the deep end. Straight away I was winning 1st division championships within years of coming to Derby, 2 or 3 years, its ironic actually cause the 1st 2 championships, I won one at Derby and I was in the Scilly Isles, Harold Wilson had told me about the Scilly Isles, I'm a big socialist actually and erm a bloke at a college once said to me "how come with you , such a big socialist, driving a Mercedes and smoking a cigar" cause I went on to my Mercedes and I started smoking when

I was about 26 . I said " the difference between you who is a Tory and me is I don't mind everybody having a bloody Mercedes and a big cigar, you bloody lot who were born with it don't want anybody else to have it". Rich people don't you know hate other people getting bloody rich and of course I was in my Mercedes with my big cigar, but I was in the Scilly Isles, Harold Wilson said to me that the Scilly Isles would suit me with the kids. So when I won it with Derby I was in the Scilly Isles.

Leeds had got done at Wolves, then when I won it at Forest I was on an aeroplane and there was a match being played and it had to be confirmed, I'd already won it before we left and the pilot was getting the scores and then he sent the girl along to tell me that we couldn't get a reception and that I'd have to wait until we got back to the airport. So I found out we had won the 2nd division and 1st division when I was in Spain, I think a few sangrias got drunk that week. I never saw the lads; I never saw them when we went away. One famous manager, I wont tell you his name because I thought he was a bit of an amateur he said " what's this business about you not training when you go away" I said " well we don't we don't do a lot" he said "well don't you think trainings essential?" I said "absolutely we train 5 weeks before the season starts, then we play Saturday, Wednesday, Saturday in European cups" I said "and come Christmas we are knackered and come Jan and Feb. I can tell the players that's been injured" he said "how can you tell that?" I said "well you can walk in the dressing room and the players that have played right up until February are white faced and the ones that have been injured, you'd think they had just come off a bloody cruise, they are full of it and never kicked a ball all season" I said "we use European matches for a break from the domestic 1st division, which was hard for us" and it was hard for us every week, hell we only had bloody 14 players and err we used to go abroad and Burnsey used to say "we are not taking any training gear are we gaffer" "no no" I said "take a pair of plimsolls and get your own shorts" and we just used to hang around the pool and soak up the sun and then we would go for a walk before our meal and that was our training for 4 days.

When we won the 2nd European cup I took them all to Spain to Cala Millor for 5 days and then we flew straight to the European cup and err we never trained one day, all we wanted was a rest, come May your on your knees, I was on my knees and I was only the manager.

BERNIE

Do you think the influx of foreigners is killing the national game?

CLOUGHIE

It's not helped, because we have now become saturated, I advocated foreigners to our football early on in my managerial career, before I thought they had something to offer, they had this typically different game with skills, we had our tackling and all that and if I could have merged the two I would have got the best team ever, so I said well let a few foreigners come in we will teach them how to tackle, and how to live and play in the conditions that we have to play football in, cause if there is a shower in Spain they put the match off you know and things like that we used to play in bloody snow. Err but it's gone overboard now.

I was with Jim Smith who was the manager of Derby County football club and he was on to me again and he said "when are you going to start coming to the matches?" "regularly "I said "the second me course is finished" he said "what course is that" I said "the one where I'm learning foreign language, I can't pronounce one bloody name of any of your players, there is 9 bloody foreigners" he said "I know what you mean" I said "if I can't pronounce one name you can't pronounce any cause you're worse than me". He had 9 in the side, 9 foreigners you see and they were from Czechoslovakia, Romania err Spain, France and all over the bloody place, and err sky television have been trying to get me back to work for 2 years now, and I keep saying to everybody who's trying to get me to work and I don't mean this rudely to you, I don't regard this as work with you cause I'm one of you. But when you've got to go on television and down to London and all that, that work takes all bloody day to get to London and all day to get back, and I work there 3 to 4 hours, so I stopped doing everything and err they have been pushing me to go back on television and do commentary, and I saw Ron Atkinson doing the Man Utd commentary one night, well I've been to Gratz cause we beat them in the European cup I think Gratz one year, but it's a different ball game now all bloody foreigners and as I say the nearest I could come to pronouncing a foreign name is spaghetti, and I like spaghetti but some of the foreigners I don't like and your lot always get a mention.

Middlesbrough lot always get a mention when I'm talking I say they go to Middlesbrough and they sign on the dotted line and they get their £20,000 left in a bank some where and they get well paid from Middlesbrough, I said and their wife's go out one morning and its pouring down and then she goes out the next morning and its snowing and she says "oh I can't live in this climate I've got to go home," the beggar we just got he's now buggered off cause of the climate.

BERNIE.

Well take Rav, Juninho and Emerson they all went, Juninho has returned now.

CLOUGHIE.

Yes , and we had a lot of time for him, you know we think you got rid of the wrong one, cause now he's come back we are delighted, is he a good player?

BERNIE.

Oh he's a quality player, no doubting that. The game against Chesterfield was going to be between 8 and 10,000, with his name on the team sheet 25,000 turned up.

CLOUGHIE

Brilliant, brilliant, my sister would have been there shouting for him.

BERNIE

Is that the one who stopped me in the bus station and said Bernie you were a good player, but not as good as my brother

CLOUGHIE

Its got to be her I've only got 2 sisters and err she's the oldest sister it's got to be her.

She used to come to Nottingham Forest with her country cousin every match my PR girl used to come to me and say your sisters here with her country cousin, I said "well I don't want to see them tell them I'm in the bath, anything." And they all used to have a fag coming from Middlesbrough they all had a bloody fag, like you know cause everybody had now't else to do up there apart from smoke, go for a pint. They would be sitting there saying "Forest's not playing very well today" and we were beating Arsenal somebody like that, you'd be in the second division as you were when I was at Forest and err then we would take on Liverpool and beat Liverpool and then we would take on all the top clubs and they used to be sitting there in the directors box saying ,"not as good as the Boro" you know and I'd say "bloody Boro, your bottom half of the 2nd division" and I used to get annoyed with them, and they enjoyed their days out, but of course I didn't mind them coming down, they were family and fantastic Boro supporters and season ticket holders simple as that, and they tell me I've never been to your new stadium, they tell me its beautiful, ehh the strides you have made since I was a player.

We used to train at a place called Hutton Road, well I used to train there and it was a trek to get from Ayersome Park to Hutton Road in fact I used to ask occasionally can I go straight to Hutton road, cause I was nearer Hutton Road than I was Ayresome Park. But there was no chance when you get in you might have a pair of boots to clean. Delapenha used to throw his boots at me and say "hey get those clean".

I became very friendly with Rolando Ugolini cause he was a character, a smashing fella he made a special effort to come and see me In Scotland last time I was there and we were playing he got on the coach and I said "hey im the bloody manager of this side" like you know. He got on the coach immaculate, he was looking around "your all on then are you" he gave it that and I'm saying bloody manager, like we were in the European cup I think. Ugolini used to book the concerts, cause there were big concerts there and Barbara used to love them, the cabarets and everything, and it was only later on in life Ugolini used to say your going, and I'd have to get 2 tickets and go on the coach, then Della used to throw his bloody boots at me and say get those done and you had to get them cleaned.

BERNIE

Did he give you a tip?

CLOUGHIE

No tip .

Oh they gave me one tip, keep off the M1 when its foggy, they gave me that one year it's the best bloody tip I got.

BERNIE.

Last question Brian; do you still have a soft spot for Middlesbrough?

CLOUGHIE

I do cause my family's there, born and bred there, you can never loose that where you are born and bred.

I phoned a guy up when he was 90 odd at Middlesbrough a school teacher called Grant and he signed me for Middlesbrough George Campsell was in charge, Grant was just an amateur when I was playing for Middlesbrough 3rd team or kids it was in those days, but Grant got my signature, and our Doreen, busy bollocks, she rang and said do you know Mr Grants 90 odd this week, and I phoned him up and he couldn't believe.

He said "I cant believe its you Bryan" well "it is" I said "I've not been up for years so I haven't seen you" he said "you sound just the same on the telephone" I said one thing I've not changed I'm still Middlesbrough through and through, born and bred Yorkshire man proud of it and I wished I was back playing for Middlesbrough.

HONOURS

BRIAN HOWARD CLOUGH

PLAYING CAREER HISTORY

1955-1961	Middlesbrough
1961-1964	Sunderland
1957-1958	England U23
1957	England B
1959	England

MANAGERIAL CAREER HISTORY

1965-1967	Hartlepool United
1967-1973	Derby County
1973-1974	Brighton and Hove Albion
1974	Leeds
1975-1993	Nottingham Forest

MANAGERIAL HONOURS (winners)

Nottingham Forest

1976-1977	Division 2 Promotion
1977-1978	League Champions
1977-1978	League Cup
1978-1979	European Cup
1978-1979	League Cup
1979-1980	European Cup
1979-1980	European Super Cup
1988-1989	League Cup
1988-1989	Simod Cup
1989-1990	League Cup
1991-1992	Zenith Data Cup

CAPS   2 Full caps for England

BRIAN CLOUGH OBE,MA

6 *But all these journalists, have been top international players. My ambition is to play a charity game against them, to see how good they really are.* **9**

On how he feels about the Press.

Take 3
Paul Gascoigne

Paul was born in Gateshead on the 27th may 1967.

Gazza joined us from Glasgow rangers back in1998 for a fee of £ 3,450,000.

There was no doubting Gazzas ability on the field but off it he had, domestic problems, and by all accounts psychological problems. Astonishingly he made his Boro debut at Wembley in the Coca Cola Cup Final at the expense of Craig Hignett. Gazza had trials with Boro as a school boy, unfortunately he was injured in a freak accident and didn't complete his trials .

Gazza played his part in gaining Boro promotion, from the 1st division, unfortunately he only showed glimpses of his old magic . On his day Gazza was one of the games great entertainers, he had the lot balance, skill, trickery , cheek, and he could create and score goals.

I met Gazza at Hurworth training ground in Darlington, in a porta cabin, he was accompanied by his son Regan.

He was open and frank in his comments and answers to my questions. I found him warm , funny and at times nervy.

The only thing I didn't like about Gazza was him gloating about beating my boyhood hero's Celtic during his stint in Glasgow with Rangers.

BERNIE

How would you briefly sum up your Boro career since you arrived?

GAZZA

Thoroughly enjoyed it, but peed off with the press. First couple of games just joined the club, it was new it wasn't as if I'd had a pre season break it was one club to another, getting to know the guys, playing a game, following few days playing another one, I was just actually trying to find my feet, before I even started the press were on my back.

BERNIE

You must be used to that?

GAZZA

Yes I'm used to that, but I told them be fair with me and I'll be fair with you. Now that I have settled, played a few games, getting to know the players and how they play and erm I'm thoroughly enjoying it at the moment.

BERNIE

Looking back at the Cup Final against Chelsea I personally thought you shouldn't have started the game.

GAZZA

I didn't want to start the game, I don't think it would have been right for me to start the game.

BERNIE

Where you fit enough to start the game?

GAZZA

I was about 70% fit to start the game, I didn't get the goals there, even if I was 120% fit I still wouldn't have wanted to play in the game. The lads got there on their own merit, I didn't think it was right me just turning up at the club and playing. Even sub I felt a little bit embarrassed at being sub, but that football I thoroughly enjoyed it. It was my first game at Wembley Coca cola so it wasn't bad.

BERNIE

Is that right on the Saturday night before the final you had a word with your room mate Paul Merson and said I'm going to give Craig Hignett my medal?

GAZZA

Er I think so.

I'm not to sure if it was that day or the morning, I think I said to Merse I had all intentions, whether it was a winners medal or a losers medal to give it to Higgy, it was just something I think he deserved it more than me .

BERNIE

How hard a decision was it joining your old rivals the old enemy, Newcastle , Middlesbrough its like joining Celtic after you played for Rangers?

GAZZA

To be fair I've been home to Newcastle and the fans have been great and just wished me all the best

BERNIE

How big an influence was Bryan Robson in you joining Boro?

GAZZA

I think it was Bryan Robson that got me to the club, I knew how big the supporters were and how disappointed they had been getting beat in 3 cup finals Robbo told me, great set up, great training ground, good bunch of lads, he said come here you'll be looked after and you'll enjoy your football. And to his word he's lived up to it I'm enjoying it now.

BERNIE

Looking at your career you left Newcastle joined Spurs, Lazio, everyone was tipping you to return to England , but eh you went to Scotland joined Rangers Why Rangers?

GAZZA

 I think if a footballer has experienced and played or went to Rangers they would know the reason why. There's not a bigger club than Rangers unless you go to the likes of Barcelona , AC Milan, the club is up there with them.

I know the Champions League was disappointing, we know that ourselves, every pre season our chairman spent a lot of money to succeed in the Champions League but we didn't have enough time to get together. Magnificent club , massive club, massive trophy cabinet and I won several winners medals up there as well.

BERNIE

You've played in a lot of big games over the years, how highly would you rate an old firm game and the atmosphere?

GAZZA

You have to witness it .

I played in 11 and was unbeaten in all 11, the one we got beat in I came on as a sub, 11 I played in unbeaten ,7 wins, 4 draws, so it was good a couple of goals, the atmosphere great.

BERNIE

Was that the best experience?

GAZZA

No Lazio and Roma is something else .

50,000 at Rangers, Lazio and Roma 100,000. But for atmosphere singing and hatred trying to out do each other I'd say Celtic would take some beating.

BERNIE

Is that right you had several threats against you in Glasgow?

GAZZA

A couple of times, I've had that before, I've had letters and death threats it can be a little worrying. I remember going to the training ground driving my car along and a guy stopped his car and rolled his window down and said watch out Gascoigne I'm going to slit your throat. Erm I didn't actually train too well that day to be fair . I get plenty of that I'm hardened to it.

BERNIE

Your Rangers career seamed to come to an abrupt end, was that a surprise? After going into a final chasing their 10th consecutive championship, I was delighted you left by the way.

GAZZA

I've left an ambitious club, to come to an ambitious club, both chairmen are willing to spend money, both have plans for the future, both of them have good sets of lads, at Rangers they were like a family to me, obviously I was hurt the way I did leave, but now its up to me to put all that behind me.

I'm still in touch with the guys, I've got my new club, new bunch of lads and they've took to me well and I've settled in very good.

BERNIE

You've been capped 54 times by England, are you happy with the tally or should it have been more?

GAZZA

I actually missed out on about 4 years of international soccer through injury, your talking about 20 or 30 games in that time.

I reckon I could have been on about 80 caps especially with the World Cup coming up and friendlys. Shame cause if I would have kept myself right and in good condition I could have reached 100 caps, it's always nice to play for your country I've passed the 50 mark which is nice, and my aim is to try and stay fit and do the business for Middlesbrough and England.

BERNIE

What would you say has been your greatest game for England?

GAZZA

One of my greatest games for England was against Czechoslovakia, a pressurized game before the 1990 World Cup , where I had to try and perform, I set up 3 and scored one which set me up and during the World Cup I enjoyed most of the games.

But the Germany game I enjoyed that, up against Matthaus, who was obviously class, and I stood up to the challenge and I enjoyed that game.

BERNIE

Do you feel any extra pressure playing for England. The press are red hot always looking at Gascoigne.

GAZZA

I don't actually find pressure playing for England, I enjoy playing for England.

What peeves me off about it is, when I was 22, 23, starting to play for England they put pressure on me to do the business for England, I was the one who had to create things, score goals, have a blinder every game and now I'm 30 and all the young kids are coming through and now its still up to me to do this and do that, so as Chris Waddle said and John Barnes, Gazza just enjoy it, when the England games come cause you don't know when your times going to come. When they say retire, get him out and all that which they are. But all these journalists have been top international players, my ambition is to play a charity game against them to see how good they really are, I'd love that.

BERNIE

You scored a terrific goal against Scotland in the European Championships, what kind of reception did you get when you returned to Ibrox?

GAZZA

A couple of Rangers players, played that day, 50, 50 the lads gave a lot of banter before hand ,when I got back every photo that was sent to get signed, I actually put them above Andy Goram's dressing room pegs, I apologise to those people who's pictures weren't returned, because Andy Goram ripped them to shreds.

BERNIE

Most people in the public eye have been stitched up from time to time, by the press ,you've been stitched up more times than most, does that frustrate you , annoy you?

GAZZA

Lucky enough to be fair they've normally given me a load of hassle and stick, you try to cope with it to the best of your ability, but I've been lucky because the public, the general public have been absolutely fantastic, no matter what the press have written ,the public have been great.

The only things that hurt me is when they start pestering my kids I think they should keep the kids out of it it's a sin when they hound them at the house and that.

BERNIE

The papers over the years they just write rubbish don't they the only thing you believe in is the date.

GAZZA

I've always said the only difference between the beano and a newspaper is 3 pence.

BERNIE

Looking towards the World Cup, has England got a realistic chance of winning it ?

GAZZA

Well erm we have got a good chance, I think we have got the players, the youth, the experience, everyone's gelling together, this thing about giving Glen Hoddle stick about mixing players and experimenting, he would rather experiment now than actually experiment in the World Cup, so like I said Graham Taylor, Bobby Robson, Terry Venables, whoever becomes manager knows that the press are going to slaughter them at the same time our own press, English people that want England to win the World Cup and their the only people who doubt us our own journalists, they hate it when England win, they absolutely hate it they can't stand it .

I mean Portugal are a very, very good team and England win the game and scored 3 great goals and did well, but we still got stick after the game so hopefully we can do it for the public of England that we do win the World Cup, Brazil are going to take some beating, but hopefully we do, and for the press hopefully well get beat for them.

BERNIE

How much faith have you got in psychologist Eileen Drury , do you think it's a good idea?

GAZZA

Eileen Drury, well when you're the England manager erm he's doing what's best for the squad, he's given everybody the opportunity to make sure that their minds are focused and er if you want to go and see her, you can if you don't you don't have too, Glens not putting anybody under any pressure, erm she's there to see if anyone wants there minds at ease, all Glen wants is for everybody to be focused on the World Cup, she's not forcing anyone to see her, she's there if you want to see her, a lot of the lads have done.

HONOURS

PAUL JOHN GASCOIGNE

PLAYING CAREER HISTORY

1985-1988	Newcastle United
1988-1992	Tottenham Hotspur
1992-1995	Lazio
1995-1998	Rangers
1998-2000	Middlesbrough
2000-2002	Everton
2002	Burnley
2003	Gansu Tianma
2004	Boston United
1987-1988	England under 21
1989	England B
1988-1998	England.

MANAGING CAREER HISTORY

Kettering Town.

PLAYING HONOURS (winners)
Tottenham

1991 FA Cup
Rangers

1996	Scottish League Champions
1997	Scottish League Champions
1996	Scottish Cup
1997	Scottish League Cup

CAPS   57 Full caps for England

' *You know the old story, you start badly and fall away.* **'**

Referring to his Boro debut.

Take 4

George Hardwick

Hardwick was one of the games most recognised post war players. He was born in Saltburn on 2nd February 1920 .George was not only noticed for his footballing ability, but also for his good looks, his nick name was gentleman George, the ladies by all account swooned over his Clarke Gable features.

He signed amateur for Middlesbrough in October 1935 and became full time professional in April 1937.

Hardwick's qualities as a left back were, he read the game well, he was a great distributor, tough tackler, all in all he was a classy defender.

I met George at the Marton Country Club, he was dressed immaculately, and was as charming as ever, although a little forgetful, he seamed sincere in everything he was saying .

It was fantastic to meet and chat with a guy who had captained Middlesbrough, England and Great Britain.

Sadly George passed away on 19th April 2004.

A true Boro great.

BERNIE

George thanks for turning up.

GEORGE

Nice to see you Bernie.

BERNIE

Is it true that in your England debut you captained the side?

GEORGE

Yes I played during the war years for about 8 or 10 times when old Joe Mercer was the captain of the England side, and I succeeded Joe as captain. My proudest moment was captaining Great Britain.

BERNIE

How many clubs did you play for?

GEORGE

Just 2 Middlesbrough and Oldham.

BERNIE

As a player you were known as Gentleman George, how did that name come about?

GEORGE

Perhaps it was the ladies that gave me that name. I remember a game when I played and we won the game and I went down to, err the room where the directors wife and daughter and friends were. I was in the middle of the room and I was talking to the chairman's daughter, suddenly she said oh my goodness, and I looked and her panties were on the floor.

BERNIE

When you were in the RAF you went 6 sparring rounds with Joe Lewis, who was the undisputed world boxing champion at the time. How did that come about?

GEORGE

Well I was based there, he was based there in the RAF its sportsmen, you can smell each other, you know if the guys a sportsman or not. Joe and I just met really, we went and visited the United States army back there and they came to the RAF base there and I and Joe talked and we met in that way. I boxed for the RAF I threatened him and he said "right we're in the gym."

BERNIE

When I arrived at Middlesbrough in 84 my first wage was £300, 12 years later certain guys are reportedly on £42,000 a week. What were you on at your Boro peak?

GEORGE

My first wage was £6, I was 17 years old, at my peak £20, with a £2 win £1 draw and I played like hell for that. In all honesty I thought you deserved better you know.

BERNIE

You had a memorable debut for Boro.

GEORGE

You know the old story; you start badly and fall away. We kicked off and they were progressing down the left side and hit this long ball into the penalty area, and I saw Bob Baxter and their number 9 going for the ball and it deflected off, and I saw this player coming in to get on the end of this deflection just inside the penalty area, and I thought right I'm covering this, and I did cover it and I got the ball and it was icy and I thought I will just turn it back to the goalkeeper, and that's what I did. The next minute that's when I heard a roar from the crowd and I looked around and David Cummings is on his hands and knees, he had slipped and the ball had trickled merrily into the far corner. As I said started badly and fell away, I kept my place anyway.

BERNIE

The Boro team you played in just before the war, was that the best Boro team ever, you did break up because of the war?

GEORGE

Yes, yes no hesitation at all there were so many good young players breathing down the necks of the big boys the internationals, that everybody was playing for their places and erm it was a real pleasure to be in that club at that time because they were so positive everybody was so sure that we were going to win the 1st division, we were going to be top in the 1st division.

BERNIE

What are you're most cherished possessions of your playing career?

GEORGE

Err the Great Britain shirt?

BERNIE

Have you still got it?

GEORGE

Yes it comes out periodically when strangers appear, or somebody wants to see it and my caps, 13 of them.

HONOURS

GEORGE HARDWICK

PLAYING CAREER HISTORY

1936-1950	Middlesbrough
1950-1956	Oldham Athletic
1947	Nations of Great Britain
	England

MANAGERIAL CAREER HISTORY

1950-1956	Oldham Athletic
1957-1959	PSV Eindhoven
1959-1961	Netherlands National Team
1964-1965	Sunderland
CAPS	13 full caps for England

' He said 'you, you ya Kangaroo bastard' like that, 'whatever your name is,' he said 'you will never be a footballer while your arsehole points to the ground'. **'**

What Jack said to Craig while on trial.

Take 5

Craig Johnston

Craig Peter Johnston was born in Johannesburg on the 8th December 1960, but lived most of his life in Australia. Craig like myself wrote a letter to Middlesbrough asking for a trial. He got his wish, but unfortunately he was rejected and returned home to Australia.

A year later his persistence paid off and he eventually signed for Middlesbrough. His debut was against Everton in a FA cup tie, in Jan 1978, aged 17.

In a 3 year period Craig played 77 games scoring 16 goals.

I met up with Craig at his home in London.

He's a bright bubbly and warm person . Who was instantly likeable.

I had only met Craig on one occasion before this interview, that was during the 1990 World Cup Finals in Italy, when he was working for Australian TV, and I was with the Republic of Ireland squad.

The funny thing was that after the interview Craig had to dash to Heathrow airport to catch a flight on a business trip, as he left the house we were still packing up the camera equipment, he said lads when your finished just close the door over, so here we were left alone in this £1 million mansion surrounded by expensive paintings, we could have been robbers for all he knew.

BERNIE

You decided to write a letter to the club asking for a trial, was that your idea?

CRAIG

I saw them on television and Middlesbrough toured, and I was in hospital err and I had a very bad leg operation.

And err I had been in hospital for about 6 months and then I saw Midddlesbrough playing.

Jack Charlton was the manager and people like Peter Brine and Stuart Boam and err Alan Foggin, now we are going back, Spike Armstrong he was bald then , he was only 17 and it really captured my imagination, err and err the fact that they were so close to me , I was in a hospital bed and I could almost see where they were playing, it was on television and err I fell in love with the concept, so I wrote to them, got my mum and dad to write to them and Manchester United and Chelsea and err Middlesbrough was the only one who wrote back. And that was Harold Shepherdson, and he said "come over if you pay your fair and your lodgings, we will see how good you are." I was there for a week and they said your no good and I had to go home, so I started crying and saying let me stay, I will prove it to you, I will prove it to you. So I paid to stay in the Medhurst and I sort of didn't get better for a long time, about a year before they discovered I was still there.

But I cleaned the boots and did the jobs the apprentices didn't want to do, so that they wouldn't tell the management that I was still hanging about.

It worked like that until Jack Charlton came and then he told me in no uncertain terms and he had a go at everyone around the dressing room. He said and "you, you ya kangaroo bastard" like that, "what ever your name is" , he said "you will never be a footballer while your arsehole points to the ground," that's what he said.

And I was convinced from that day, that I would prove this guy wrong. I would prove to him that I could play. About a year after Charlton had left and John Neal took over . I had 2 or 3 games for the 1st team and played really well and err the newspaper said Jack Charlton said I always knew he would be good . So he claimed responsibility .

BERNIE

You made your Boro debut against Everton in 1978. Any memories of that debut?

CRAIG

Two memories that stand out are the 1st time that I was ever a footballer, which was what we are talking about the Everton match, the 2nd one was scoring in the FA Cup final against Everton again, so it means a dreadful lot to me. I mean I could have never have played football ever again after those 2 or 3 moments, where I stood out there and said "its me and you know" You have the crowd and the ball comes to you and you do something and kick it and then the crowd responds to the kick and you think, wow what a buzz, hard to explain you know, you know how it works.

BERNIE

Was Graeme Souness a bit of an idol for you?

CRAIG

Yes absolutely, err absolutely, he was a total inspiration. I was his boot boy and I think he remembered fondly the trip to Austria, so he actually looked after me, he made it his business to look after me and make sure that nobody was really taking the mickey out of me.

BERNIE

Was he one of the tough lads?

CRAIG

Souness was the tough lad, he was the kiddie, the organiser, the general on and off the field.

And he had a lot to do with the style of Middlesbrough in those days.

So when he left for Liverpool he fixed me up with his digs and the famous Feebie Haig down on Chipchase. Err and Alan Murray was part of that gang and I stayed there for 2 or 3 years and they really looked after me incredibly well.

BERNIE

What would you say your game was all about, was it pace , skill , work rate or a mixture, obviously you worked hard at your game.

CRAIG

It was the defences I always had was, skill and tactical awareness and the football intelligence and they are very tangible Things that great players posses . And because I didn't have any of them, in any particular quantity, I worked on pace, aggression, team work, supplying who ever was on the ball with another option, unselfish runs and err I was accused of been a little bit tunnel vision cause now and again , I used to try a little bit of fancy stuff, because that's what I admired in football that's what I didn't have.

Now and again I would come unstuck, but err I think over the years I developed from watching good players, one or two err tricks and I improved, err so I was always pinching myself, that I was in the company of such good players at Middlesbrough and Liverpool.

But I've got no hang ups as to how good or bad I was, I always thought I was lucky to be there.

BERNIE

After playing 77 games for Middlesbrough, scoring 16 goals, Liverpool wanted your signature, were you surprised it was Liverpool?

CRAIG

Err it was funny because, the team at the time wasn't Liverpool, it was Brian Clough and Nottingham Forest. So they had come in 1st and then Spurs and Man Utd, but nobody took any notice of Man Utd, but I did and then Liverpool came in .

And the Liverpool connection was that Souness, err used to call back regularly to Chipchase and Feebie and I said jokingly , if they need a new midfielder down there give me the nod , so he phoned me up and said they had approached him already, err and they were thinking of replacing Terry McDermott, and would I be interviewed. I had to find Cloughie and Cloughie was on holiday in France, and I couldn't get hold of him.

So I went to Liverpool and err I was ready to sign, and I said "but I have to do one thing," which was to find Cloughie, cause I said I would, and I tracked him down and err, he was the man behind Forest.

So I thought I was signing for a man, rather than Liverpool the institution, and I thought this is not Bob Paisley I'm signing for, it's that institution, that academy, that heritage, and I had already been fascinated by the Shankley thing and the Scottish sum in Liverpool, and I guess that's what swung it. But err Cloughie wasn't a happy man let me tell you.

BERNIE

Between 81 and 88 at Anfield, you won 5 league titles, FA Cup, 2 league cups, European cup. What was your proudest moment?

CRAIG

All of the above I guess.

BERNIE

You designed the very successful Adidas predator boot, how did that idea come about?

CRAIG

When I retired I said I would never get involved in the game again, cause I'd played for Middlesbrough and Liverpool and got the medals, I had done that thing. Someone knocked on my door, a couple of kids with a ball under their arm, and said 'err Mr Johnston could you come and coach our team we are not very good,' so then I was hooked, I was back into football.

So I coached the team and they were right, they weren't very good. I think in 12 games we had 11 losses. Anyway during one of the coaching sessions, I was telling them how to swerve the ball, and I said "you have got to grip the ball and pick it up with your boot, so grip it like a table tennis bat," "But Mr Johnston, its raining and the balls slippery so its not like a table tennis bat." And bing I had an idea, so I went home and got a table tennis bat, put it on the wet leather boots and went out in the rain, and it chipped more, and I said "bing I'm on to something."

So I followed it through, spent a fortune, fortune on it got a patent, and took it to Nike and Reebok, both knocked it back.

Then I took it to Adidas and they signed it on, and while I was there, I was there for 2 years living in Germany, I created the traction sole and spearheaded all the development of the World Cup ball.

HONOURS

CRAIG PETER JOHNSTON

PLAYING CAREER HISTORY

1977-1981	Middlesbrough
1978	Newcastle KB United
1981-1988	Liverpool
1982	Newcastle KB United
1981	England under 21

PLAYING HONOURS (winners)
Liverpool

1982	Division 1 level 1
1983	Division 1 level 1
1983	Football league cup
1984	Football league cup
1984	European Cup
1984	Division 1 level 1 ,
1986	Division 1 level 1
1986	FA Cup
1986	Charity Shield (shared)
1988	Division 1 level 1

' *I felt very upset to leave, but I think at the time it was the best thing for me, and the club.* **'**

On leaving after relegation.

00 5074

Take 6
Juninho

Oswaldo Giroldo Junior was born in Sao Paulo on 22nd February 1973. He arrived in October 1995 from Sao Paulo for a fee of £ 4.75 million. Juninho was the greatest player I've witnessed since I arrived on Teesside in 1984/85.

Despite his lack of height, he had the heart the size of a lion, he was light and nimble, possessed great balance, was highly skilful and could create and score goals.

I had originally pencilled in an interview with Juninho over in Spain while he was playing for Atletico Madrid.

Unfortunately I failed to make it because of my flying phobia.

Eventually I met him at Crathorne Hall Hotel on the outskirts of Yarm. This was my opportunity to ask him to his face a couple of queries I had raised on the radio. To his credit he never ducked a question. I found him sincere, warm, and friendly, with no edge all in all he was a nice guy.

Juninho played a major part in winning the clubs one and only trophy The Carling Cup.

BERNIE

You signed for boro in 1995 for £4.75 million, what attracted you to Teesside and how big a part did Bryan Robson play to get you here?

JUNINHO

When I was playing in Sao Paulo, er it was just 2 years, the biggest club in Brazil, so I never thought I would be going out.

When I played for Brazil in the Umbro cup that was when Bryan Robson had an interest in me, so he came to me and start talking about the English game and about the clubs ambition, so he was a big name in the world, so I believed in him and I trusted him so I came here.

BERNIE

Other big names arrived Ravanelli, Emerson. How good were both of them to play alongside, to play with?

JUNINHO

Friendly and he is a good player as well, a great player Ravanelli .Well Emerson I didn't know him before he came here so, his movement helped me a lot. Because always when I had the ball, I always had an option to play to him because he had great movement both players, not just both players but other players helped me a lot to adapt to English football.

BERNIE

In your 1st season you only scored 2 goals, but you created the majority for others. Does that give you as much pleasure? Making a goal as to scoring a goal?

JUNINHO

Yes, yes I prefer making scoring goals, then I score goals I've never been a good goal scorer, a goal scorer. I prefer to make opportunities to score, of course I think at this moment, in the football a lot of people see who score the goals, not who did passes to him to score goal, I always look for the player that make the other player to score, because sometime just to put the ball in the net that's our job, and you just put the ball in the net and you have a name not him, so the people have to think more about this.

BERNIE

I wished I had played alongside you.

In your 2nd season you really turned on the style, in fact the fans voted you their greatest player of all time, you must have been delighted with that?

JUNINHO

Yes, yes, I was very glad to, er I just had played my 2nd year how I was playing in Brazil, so I enjoy here. All the players when they had the ball looked for me to pass to so that helped me a lot and I had a confidence with all the players, I didn't do that alone if it wasn't for my team mates I didn't get it.

BERNIE

The public say that the team you played in was the most attractive and the best. What went wrong, 2 cup finals nothing no silverware, relegation?

JUNINHO

It was a very exciting season, I think we had a better team than most that stayed in the premier league, I don't know in that time when we played in the cup games they were crucial games, either you win or you were out , so I don't know we had to concentrate more in the cup games, that was why we got to 2 cup finals, we had a great team as well I think, in the league games if you lose one game we thought oh live for the next one, next one we'll have a chance to win and in the end we had no chance to save it. I think that's what happened err it was a very strange season so I can't explain what happened.

BERNIE

After the FA Cup final most of the players returned for the reception, you didn't, a lot of people were disappointed with that. You know I was thinking number one player where is he, were you so disappointed that you didn't return?

JUNINHO

That's a good question, because I didn't know that the people were upset with me, because I explained to Bryan and the directors, that my mama had a operation and she was in Brazil, so I was worried, so before the cup final game I had my ticket booked, then after the game I wanted to get to Brazil as soon as possible to see my mama, that's why I didn't come.

BERNIE

When the club was relegated you were the 1st player to leave, and I accused you of jumping ship, in other words you left you were the 1st player to leave why did you have to leave so quickly?

JUNINHO

Well that's why I had a lot of meetings with the president, (chairman) and Bryan. Atletico and some other clubs wanted to buy me, and I had an opportunity to play in the world cup, I think for anyone who wants to play in the world cup, I think to play in the England 1st division. My chance to play in the world cup would have been minimal, so I explained this to Steve Gibson and Bryan Robson and they had a plan to sell me for good money, to do good business for the club, and that's what happened, not just because I wanted to leave, I think both me and the club and Atletico agreed this negociation.

BERNIE

If I had been the manager I would have kept you despite what your pleas were. Rav and Emerson also left and as a result the team lost its flair and glamour, did no one ever give a thought to the fans, Bryan Robson or Steve Gibson. Yourself left followed by Ravanelli and Emmerson did none of you think hold on here, do I have to go, you know 3 of you came and went within a 2 year period?

JUNINHO

Well err my heart was here, when I came here I came to help a team to become big and to win something and we didn't , so when I left I missed something so that's why I'm here. I can't talk about Emerson and Rav I just think all the players had ambition. I felt very upset to leave, but I think at that time it was the best thing for me and for the club as well.

BERNIE

I've nothing against any nationality, but a lot of overseas players are classed as mercenaries

Is that an unfair comment? I'm against nobody but I just feel there's a lot coming into the country just for the money.

JUNINHO

My opinion, I think if you had in Brazil better organisation and better conditions to play I think most players wouldn't leave Brazil , but there is a very big difference the organisation here, the opportunities and the conditions, the conditions is important, it is important like any professional if you have a better job and better money in another country we go there, because you have to think of your future and your family and give them a good life and what most of the Brazilian players, not only Brazilian players but also South American players,come to England because of better organisation and better conditions to play.

BERNIE

What difference did you find when you joined Atletico compared to Middlesbrough, was the football even more physical than the English game?

JUNINHO

Not more physical, more tactical game than English football, here you enjoy playing, you don't enjoy playing a more tactical game. When I played at Boro in my 1st game I got help, with the Boro my movements were free, in Atletico with Rio Zanka now Rito Ranyers they limit a player on the pitch so that's why I found it difficult to play .

BERNIE

You have never hidden your love for Boro and the fans, but did you actually talk to Leeds and Aston Villa and why if you're so much in love with Boro, there were pictures in the papers.

JUNINHO

That picture gave me a lot of problems in Madrid as well, so with Leeds I didn't talk to Leeds. True I went to Villa park to talk to the president, because when Atletico decided to sell me because the manager doesn't want me in the team, 1st team that came to Atletico and Atletico said to me look you have got an opportunity make sure it's a good club make sure you feel comfortable to go there, because I had to leave Atletico, I didn't like to just sit on the bench just to watch the games and the president said to me "its better you leave this manager don't make you play." So Middlesbrough showed interest but before, when I started to have problems with Rio Zanka, I started off the season and after when I had problems with Ranieri, Middlesbrough didn't come and they didn't say anything , that's why I was worrying Aston Villa came that's why I came to England, to see who was interested.

BERNIE

Did you have to give it a lot of thought to come and join on loan, surely a player of your quality who had proved it?

JUNINHO

That's what Middlesbrough and Atletico had agreed, so I just wanted to leave and go to a place where I could play. I'm not happy with this aggrement, so I'd like to know what will happen to me, I'd like to stay here I'd like to wait until the end of the season to see if I stay or go back ,I make my decision so err if the negotiating can be sorted that will be better for me.

BERNIE

At this minute in time your playing in a number of games are you enjoying it?

JUNINHO

Yes I'm enjoying it I've found a different team and different players, I think we are a better team than before, we have to prove it on the pitch, we haven't as yet, but we have a better team than we had then, but err the way im playing now I'm comfortable, its different from last time, we are with the ball Bryan gives me a licence to movement and to receive the ball wherever I want on the pitch, so that's a little bit different from last time, I need more time to adapt, it's a different game now I have to help more than I did last time. So I just take my time to adapt, not just Juninho but all the players are looking to get better.

BERNIE

At this minute in time your playing right side, of the 3 in midfield, if you had a choice to play there or in the hole behind the front 2, where would you like to play?

JUNINHO

In the hole behind the 2 strikers. I don't know how to defend, I'm learning, Bryan put me there in the midfield 3 and I have to be a player that can play more than one position, I have to adapt to a different position that's what im looking to achieve.

BERNIE

If you had a wish for the millennium what would it be?

JUNINHO

First to keep my whole family together, that's my personal wish and professionally to get into the Middlesbrough history, to win something, all the supporters will enjoy a lot if we win something.

HONOURS

OSWALDO GIROLDO JR

PLAYING CAREER HISTORY

1993-1995	Sao Paulo
1995-1997	Middlesbrough
1997-2002	Atletico Madrid
1999-2000	Middlesbrough
2000-2001	Vasco da Gama
2002	Flamengo
2002-2004	Middlesbrough
2004-2005	Celtic
2005-2006	Palmeiras
2007	Flamengo
2007-2008	Sydney FC
1995-2002	Brazil

PLAYING HONOURS (winners)

Brazil

2002 World Cup

Sao Paulo

1993	Copa Libertadores
1993	Supercopa Sudamericana
1993	Interconential Cup
1994	Recopa Sudamericana
1994	Copa Conmebol
1995	Brazilian Champions Cup

Vasco da Gama

2000	Campeonato Brasileiro Serie A
2000	Copa Mercosur

Middlesbrough

2004 League Cup

Flamengo

2007	Taca Guanabara
2007	Campeonato Carioca
CAPS	68 Full caps for Brazil

6 *When I signed for Middlesbrough, I got a £10 signing on fee.* **9**

Wilf on joining his home town club.

00 5074

Take 7
Wilf Mannion

Wilf Mannion was born at Southbank on 16th May 1918.

Wilf signed for Middlesbrough from non league club South bank back in August 1936. Wilfs nickname was the golden boy. The first sighting of wilf in a Boro shirt came in January 1937 against Portsmouth, the game ended 2-2. He went on to score over 100 goals for his home town club a phenomenal strike rate when you consider he was a winger.

His greatest performance was against Blackpool, when he scored 4 goals in a 9-2 drubbing of the Tangerines.

Long before I interviewed him, I used to have a drink and a meal with him before the home games in the Mannion box.

I found him warm, funny and charming.

I met up with Wilf at the Riverside Stadium to do the interview. The golden boy was accompanied by his best mate Albert Lanny, while doing the interview Lanny would intervene and refresh his memory, they were a tremendous double act.

I have to say it was a great pleasure, to meet arguably the greatest ever player to wear the red shirt of Middlesbrough.

When I signed for Middlesbrough back in 1984, my father said to me try and meet Wilf Mannion, he is one of the greatest ever players, not just for Middlesbrough, but for England as well. Thankfully I achieved it.

Sadly Wilf passed away on 14th April 2000.

BERNIE

Welcome Wilf and Lanny to Boro TV, Wilf how does it feel being Middlesbrough's most famous player?

WILF

Well it scares me, because there were great players all around me, you know like Matthews, Finney and Lawton, you know you had to be right on top of your game with them.

BERNIE

You signed for Middlesbrough in September 1936, who was it that signed you?

WILF

Wilf Gillow, I was on the running track and he stopped me on the running track, he said "You have been picked to go to South Africa for 3 months, but you're not going to go I have already agreed with the football association that you are going to have complete rest." I couldn't stop running. When I signed for Middlesbrough I got a £10 signing on fee.

BERNIE

So what were you on at the peak of your career?

WILF

£10, £9 and £8.

BERNIE

You made your Boro debut in January 1937, in a 2-2 draw against Portsmouth at Ayresome Park, can you remember anything about that game?

WILF

I remember a great player that played for the Pompey, Dickinson, he played for England. I tore them to shreds really, I used to do certain things and I could walk back after crucifying them.

BERNIE

Just as you took hold of a regular 1st team spot, success seamed just around the corner but was intervened and you lost 6 full seasons of top flight football. How frustrating was this?

WILF

Very much so. I was with a famous cricketer as well; he got bombed out with me, on the Catalina planes when the war intervened. Edward Veriton was the greatest bowler in the world of cricket he was and I was his runner. It didn't affect me much I went straight in and played a game of soccer, I loved the game, you know went crackers about it.

BERNIE

What was your finest hour in a Boro shirt?

WILF

Against Blackpool at Ayresome Park

Bernadette my wife was there, I put on a show an excellent one and I did everything out of this world, controlling going to the half way line, at the end of the game they all stood and actually applauded me going off the pitch after the game, they had about 8 internationals, it's still talked about today.

BERNIE

People described you as the golden boy of football, with the great body swerve and you were a genius, was that all natural ability or did you work at it?

WILF

All natural, I played 19 years for Middlesbrough and never got caught out once on my legs, never in all my career did I get caught, only time when I got caught, was when I climbed for a high ball, I used to sit in the air, the other fellow played for Scotland Billy Liddle outside left, when I started to drop he started to climb and he broke my cheekbone.

BERNIE

When Boro signed Juninho people said he was the new Wilf Mannion, is that a fair assessment?

WILF

No he is always getting caught too much and at the end of his run, he is not doing anything at all, I never got caught at all never got touched.

BERNIE

How are you enjoying life at the moment?

WILF

Very good, I see the Boro every fortnight.

BERNIE

Thanks very much for joining me Wilf.

WILF

Thanks very much Bernie.

HONOURS

WILFRED JAMES MANNION

PLAYING CAREER HISTORY

1936-1954	Middlesbrough
1954-1956	Hull City
1956-1958	Cambridge United
1946-1951	England

CAPS   26 Full caps for England

**'I don't know why.
Cause of the
amount of drink
I used to
drink and
not fall down. '**

On why he was called
the Magic Man.

Take 8
Paul Merson

The Magic Man was born in Harlsden London on the 20th March 1968.

He linked up with Middlesbrough after moving for a fee of £4.5 million on the 7th July 1997. He was brought in to replace Juniniho who had left for Atletico.

The question was could he fill the Brazilians boots. The answer was yes he did, he had cheek, ability, skill and was a creator and a taker of goals.

In fact it was his performances and goals, which gained us promotion back into the top flight.

I met up with Merse at the Tall Trees in Yarm; the interview took place at the side of the swimming pool under a fake palm tree. Merse was dressed like a turkey; he was wrapped in what looked like a tin foil jacket (he must have purchased it in London).

I found Paul to be hesitant and aloof but still enjoyed a laugh. This was my 1st of many Bernie's Abouts.

BERNIE

How's things gone since you joined Middlesbrough from Arsenal?

MERSE

Don't think they could have gone any better, so far top of the league and had a good cup run and that's the thing really as long as we go up and at the moment we are top.

BERNIE

What about your goal haul, 14 goals, what's your best at Arsenal?

MERSE

16 plus, that was in my 1st season at Arsenal so don't expect anything after this year.

BERNIE

I must ask you about those red boots you wear, where did you get those a car boot sale?

MERSE

My boot company made them and wanted me to wear them, because of the red Boro kit, but they are comfortable and hopefully all the kids will be wearing them soon.

BERNIE

How proud were you to captain the England B team?

MERSE

Captaining the England B team was a great honour for me, its any kids dream, you know it doesn't matter if it's A B or C as Nigel Pearson says F or E or whatever, but err no I was very pleased.

What I won years ago, those things have gone now you can't keep on living on them.

BERNIE

You were quoted as saying Emerson was a big loss when he departed, no mention of Ravanelli, so you didn't miss him?

MERSE

We miss Emmo very much, you know he was an outstanding player and you know, his presence on the pitch, you know, it was worth a goal really, so we miss him, and I was disappointed when he went and how easily he with Rav, I don't think he was missed, he was bad for team spirit, he was all for himself and err you know, I wouldn't have signed if he was still here, I made that clear. He was let go. But err

BERNIE

How big a wrench was it leaving Arsenal?

MERSE

No it wasn't really.

It was a challenge to come up to Middlesbrough, they had just dropped down another division and err it was just a big challenge really.

BERNIE

People questioned your ambition, did that hurt at the time?

MERSE

Yes it did really, cause people were saying I'd come up for the money and this and that, but people at Arsenal will tell you, the difference up here to my wages down in Arsenal is not very much at all.

What I got offered at Arsenal was not far off this, and that's why people were surprised that I left Arsenal to come to Middlesbrough, cause there wasn't that much difference in wages.

BERNIE

How did you get the nickname the magic man, obviously it came from Arsenal?

MERSE

I don't know really, I think it was off the radio, a man called Jonathan Pearce, David Rocastle Called me it years ago, when we were at Arsenal, I don't know why, cause of the amount of drink I used to drink and not fall down I think.

BERNIE

Talking about Arsenal, how sweet was it scoring against your old team for Middlesbrough

MERSE

It was nice to score against Arsenal but the result wasn't good. It was nice to score but I think second half we did ourselves proud, but first half, it was a bit embarrassing really.

BERNIE

Your biggest goal must be a return to the premiership, but you must be looking to the world cup, especially after your performance for the England B side.

MERSE

Yes I've put myself in a better position after the B game than before it obviously, but I've got to continue to play well for Middlesbrough. And my 1st aim is to go up with Middlesbrough football club.

The world cup lasts for a month or 2, but I'm here for 5 years, and I don't really want to be playing in division 1 for too much longer.

BERNIE

How important is skipper Nigel Pearson?

MERSE

He is very important to the team, you know when Nigel's not playing, we seam to struggle and he's missed badly every time he doesn't play. The more games he is fit for the more chance we have of going up

BERNIE

What initially attracted you to Teesside, Juninho had just left Ravanelli was going to depart, why did you join?

MERSE

I thought it was a great challenge.

I think first of all when someone like Bryan Robson comes in for you, who personally to me is a legend in football, err it just shows you, think how that kind of man wants you to play for his football team and the challenge was to get Middlesbrough up into the premier, and that's what I done, I'm not being big headed, but I think if I didn't go there, there weren't to many other people queuing up to get there.

I have no qualms I went there and I did a job, then I left under a cloud, which is a shame really, cause a lot of people should look and think, well we wouldn't be in the premier now, and that's not being big headed that's just being honest.

BERNIE

Did you feel a certain pressure, as if it was your job to get us back in the premier league, you were a big signing?

MERSE

Yes definitely, it was all on my shoulders, definitely all on my shoulders, you know I don't look at it any other way, you know I had to come in and fill a stars boots in Juninho that everybody loved, you know and that was the hardest thing to do, and err I done that definitely, everything was down to me, if we never went up it was my fault and that's the way it is, that's football. They paid a lot of money for me, it would have been my fault if we never got promoted, I would have stayed.

BERNIE

You would have?

MERSE

Yes I would have stayed, but I feel my job was done and I never let anybody down.

BERNIE

A lot of things were said on your departure, do you regret your comments?

MERSE

I never said them.

So you know things where put in the paper that I didn't say and people believed them, you know, err I left because I was homesick mainly and I didn't tell the players what to do and how to run their life go out and have a drink, they can do that and I can do that, players weren't drinking in the dressing room, you know, so I never said them things, that someone said I did but everybody believes I did. You have got to understand my wife and kids live down in London and you know at the end of the day football comes second to that.

BERNIE

Last season Bryan Robson came in for a bit of criticism, you gave him your full support in the media, why did you do that?

MERSE

Cause if Bryan Robson ain't there no one will play for them, that's my personal opinion.

People go there because Bryan Robson is the manager, he draws players there,

Alen Boksich wouldn't be playing there if Bryan Robson wasn't the manager, Karembeu wouldn't be there. Bryan Robson carries the name of Middlesbrough football club, and I think people have to understand that he is a big, big name, I can't talk highly enough of him, I think he was an outstanding manager.

HONOURS

PAUL CHARLES MERSON

PLAYING CAREER HISTORY

1985-1997	Arsenal
1997	Brentford
1997-1998	Middlesbrough
1998-2002	Aston Villa
2002-2003	Portsmouth
2003-2006	Walsall
2006	Tamworth
1988-1990	England U21
1991-1998	England B
1991-1998	England

MANAGERIAL CAREER HISTORY

2004-2006	Walsall

PLAYING HONOURS (winners)

Arsenal

1989	League Championship
1991	League Championship
1993	FA Cup
1993	League Cup
1994	European winners cup

CAPS	21 Full caps for England

6 *It doesn't matter what game of football you're in, if you are champions in that particular league, you know you've achieved something special.* **9**

On winning.

Take 9

Bobby Murdoch

Bobby was born in Bothwell Lanarkshire on 17th August 1944.

After 14 years at Glasgow Celtic, he moved south and joined Middlesbrough in the1973-4 season- no fee was involved.

His league debut was against Bristol City and he marked the occasion with a stunning goal

In1975 he was appointed youth team coach and when John Neal departed, he became manager in 1981, with no previous managerial experience.

I travelled to Bobby's house in Glasgow, picked him up and headed to Paradise (Celtic Park) to do the interview in the away dug out.

Before our chat Bobby gave us a guided tour of the trophy room. The one question that I had to ask Bobby off camera, was something that had wrangled with me for years as a kid the rumours had been rife that Celtic manager Jock Stein had a tattoo of King William of orange on his chest. I was delighted that Bobby quashed the rumours by saying it was utter nonsense.

I found Bobby a typical Glaswegian, down to earth, welcoming and warm, it was a great pleasure to meet one of my boyhood hero's.

Sadly Bobby passed away on 15th May 2001.

BERNIE.

Started with Celtic, was that always an ambition to play for the club, either Celtic or Rangers coming from Glasgow.

BOBBY

Regarding Celtic I was brought up as a Celtic fan, I went straight to Celtic football club as a school boy so I've known nothing else, but err football

BERNIE

When I was a young lad my father used to rant and rave about this guy called Bobby Murdoch. When I was brought up Kenny Dalglish was my idol. Did you have any boyhood heroes?

BOBBY

Well I would think that probably the team that beat Rangers in the league cup final, in 1957 they won 7-1 There where a lot of good players in that team, the likes of Neil Mochan who was associated with Middlesbrough, Bobby Collins, Billy McPhail, Charlie Tully, Bobby Evans, you know, Bertie Peacock erm I mean I could name the full team. They where my heroes at that time.

BERNIE

You had 14 glorious years at Parkhead .Tell us a bit about your successes and what you actually won.

BOBBY

Well err, what I actually won was err, 8 championship medals in a row, missed out on the 9th that's because I joined Middlesbrough. (laughs)

But anyway we won the 2nd division the next year. You can say that's 9 in a row and 8 league cup medals, I think its 5 winners and 3 losers.

In the Scottish cup I played in 7 of them and I think I had 4 winners plus Glasgow cup winners, few caps and of course the European cup.

BERNIE

You clinched promotion winning the championship in your 1st season in Teesside .How did that compare to your honours in Glasgow.

BOBBY

It's the same feeling you're the champions. Its great because the squad we had at Middlesbrough, everybody enjoyed each others company, training was great, then again we had won it by Easter time or something like that so there was a lot of celebration.

A lot of people put a lot of hard work into that. The people who were involved in the coaching side, training side, big Jack, so for us as players it was a great achievement

How it worked out for me funnily enough I didn't know what I was putting myself into, but I was impressed by big Jack and what he had told me about the area and things like that you know, in the end I was there, err 9 and a half years . But its just the same feeling as going out at Celtic Park and doing a bit, you know, winning championships the feelings the same all over. It doesn't matter what game of football your in if you're the champions in that particular league you know you've achieved something special, then again the Middlesbrough fans were begging for it as well they were very good to me I got on well with them.

BERNIE

Jack Charlton signed you. How was your relationship with big Jack?

BOBBY

Err it was you take Jack for what he is.

He took me for what I was. We had a great relationship, we would talk and go out and have a couple of beers and chat about things. But when it was about work it was work, we respected each other and what we were trying to achieve, so we got on quite well.

There was only one occasion when he had just arrived, he was looking for a grouse beater. He took me up to the moors gave me a big stick and a pair of Wellingtons and I had to go about beating the ground All that Jack did was go about with his gun . I never fell for that again.

BERNIE

In 1981 after John Neal's departure, you stepped up into the hot seat as manager. How did you enjoy that experience?

BOBBY

It was err, obviously, I wanted to do it but erm I was never happy .

I don't think that the fact that we had lost so many players, there was no pressure on me from the board or anything it was just that a few players left at that time, youth players who I had worked with in the youth system and other players, at that time there was freedom of contract. I think they had to be offered contracts 3 months before their contract expired, err the previous manager never did anything like that.

I remember going to old Trafford to a tribuneral with Mark Proctor, but he had already been listed by Nottingham Forest because he played with Clough and Taylor in a youth tournament in Tenerife, but err I'm not going to say what they had done over there but he was in his legal rights and player after player were going to resign

I had no chance of negotiating before because I didn't know if I was getting the job or not, so everything was left in vain. By that time I got us relegated and then it wasn't too clever in the 1st half of the 2nd season. It was just too much for me. Anyway they did the right thing and sacked me.

BERNIE

Was there any financial backing at that time?

BOBBY

No I signed a few players they weren't good enough I got into a nose dive and couldn't get out of it.

BERNIE

Do you think the players these days are better than the Murdochs, Jimmy Johnstones the Sounesses. The wages, the signing on fees, would make you think they are.

BOBBY

No their not as good as us.

The reason is they get the money before they kick a ball. They're not hungry, they go through the motions; they try to get each other into trouble on the park.

When we played it was men that played, it was men against men. But we had to be playing before we earned any money. But nowadays they can get all this sponsorship and these wages, no the games gone down hill.

BERNIE

Well Bobby thanks very much for talking to us.

BOBBY

My pleasure Bernie

BERNIE

Hope to see you on Teesside.

BOBBY

Give my regards to all the players down there and my friends and relations. It was nice to speak to you.

HONOURS

BOBBY MURDOCH

PLAYING CAREER HISTORY
1959-1973   Celtic
1973   Middlesbrough

MANAGING CAREER HISTORY
1981-1982 Middlesbrough.

PLAYING HONOURS (winners)
Celtic
1967 European Cup

1965-1966	League Cup
1965-1967	League Championship
1965-1967	League Championship
1965-1966	League Cup
1966-1967	League Cup
1966-1967	League Championship
1966-1967	League Cup
1967-1968	League Cup
1967-1968	League Cup
1967-1968	League Championship
1968-1969	League Championship
1968-1969	League Cup
1969-1970	League Cup
1969-1970	League Championship
1969	Scottish Cup
1970-1971	League Championship
1971-1972	League Championship
1971	Scottish Cup
1972-1973	League Championship
1972	Scottish Cup

Middlesbrough
1973/ 74   Football League 2nd division

CAPS   12 Full caps for Scotland

'I don't mean any offence or disrespect, but the reason we lost the League Cup lies entirely with Bryan Robson. '

On why Boro lost the League Cup.

Take 10

Fabrizio Ravenelli

Fabrizio Ravanelli signed from Juventus in July 1996, for a fee of £7m, he settled into life on Teesside instantly, scoring a hat-trick in his premier league debut against Liverpool, his nickname was the white feather and his goal celebration and trademark was the best I have witnessed, pulling his shirt over his head after every goal, exposing his well toned torso.

After scoring 31 goals in 1996- 97 season, he departed and joined Marseille.

I travelled to Rome to meet the white feather at Lazio's training ground.

I met up with him in the training ground.

When I witnessed the facilities, I could understand his criticism of Boro. I awaited his arrival, Rav pulled up in his Ferrari, jumped out casually. He was smartly dressed, eyes camouflaged with a pair of designer glasses, we shook hands and carried on with the interview.

Rav for me was a colourful character, confident, outspoken and at times outrageous, his English was limited therefore I needed a translator, Sergio travelled with us from Middlesbrough in fact he studied in Middlesbrough and was a relation of Ravs, small world don't you think.

BERNIE

You did not make your Serie A debut until the age of 24. Why did it take you so long?

RAVANELLI.

Well because in those days football was different, at the end of the 80s and the beginning of the 90s it was difficult for young football players to play in the Serie A. At the age of 20 there were few young players around. Now it's all changed, now young players are given a chance quite easily by clubs.

BERNIE

You went to Juventus in 1992. Would you class that as a dream move?

RAVANELLI.

Yes, it was a dream at that time, now a days and in the history of football, Juventus have always been one of the greatest clubs in Italy and in the world.

I used to support Juventus so it was a fantastic dream move. I remember my 1st day there, I was sweating and shaking, very, very nervous, playing alongside the likes of Vialli, Kola, Chesnay, Roberto Baggio and David Platt was fantastic. I settled in gradually and then established myself as a 1st team player, the time at Juventus was very satisfactory for me.

BERNIE.

You scored in the European cup final. Was that the highlight of your club career?

RAVANELLI.

Talking about that at this very moment sends shivers down my spine.

It had always been a dream to score in the champion's league final, as we were progressing through the rounds having scored already 5 goals in that competition, I was thinking all the time about playing and maybe scoring in the final.

I knew that we would play the final in Rome, in the Olympic stadium, with a fantastic atmosphere similar to Wembley, therefore that goal stands as one of the greatest moments in my career and I hope to have the chance one day to do it again.

I am in great shape now and hope to keep playing like I am at present and hopefully win trophies with Lazio, like I did with Juventus

BERNIE.

Where did the nickname the white feather come from, or is it obvious?

RAVANELLI

Because of my hair, but also because when Bettega, one of my idols, used to play for Juventus he also had grey hair and this nickname. They associated my image with Bettega, and gave me the nickname White feather.

BERNIE.

You left Juventus and joined boro for a fee of 7 million. Why did you come to Teesside, was it money or ambition?

RAVANELLI

No it wasn't for money even though it is something important for a football player.

It was a fancy of mine, I had always been captain at Juventus, I had played many important games, like for instance in the Bernabeu stadium in front of 120,000 spectators, I was a very important player a protagonist .

One day Mr Rayends the Juventus and fiat chairman rang me up saying I would be the future of Juventus the new captain I was so happy. Then in the summer while I was on holiday I was reading in the papers that I was about to sign for Middlesbrough Juventus wouldn't tell me anything, they had already agreed everything without even informing me. I was very disappointed then when the Boro representative came to talk to me in Milan, I totally believed everything Bryan Robson, whom I hold in high esteem said to me, my only mistake was not seeing for myself before signing , the training facilities and the training methods at Boro.

They told me that Boro would be a success story, a new force in the English premiership and in Europe like Parma in Italy, but things worked out to be not as they were represented to me.

BERNIE

You scored a hat-trick against Liverpool in your Middlesbrough debut , is that your best ever debut?

RAVANELLI.

I also scored a hat-trick on my debut for Raggiana against Arona , it wasn't the 1st time I'd scored a hat-trick on my debut, but I think to score at Liverpool was surely the most important , my very first game in England in a different league and country , yes a sensational debut.

BERNIE

You forged a great partnership with Juninho, how good was Juninho?

RAVANELLI

He is a fantastic player, I don't know why he did not have success in Spain, because I rate Juninho as one of the best footballers in the world. It was very important for me to play alongside him, many of the goals I scored were Juninho's merit . He is a wonderful player and a very good person , I think in order to exploit to the maximum his skills, you have to play him in a position that suits him.

BERNIE.

Some people said that Juninho and Emerson were the only two players on the same wavelength as yourself , would you agree?

RAVANELLI

Well there were many important players in that squad , not only me Juninho and Emerson, we were obviously the most well known.

I was a bit disappointed when Nick Barmby was sold, he was a very talented footballer who played for the team, who could have provided me with loads of assists and great goals.

There were other important players who worked hard like Robbie Mustoe maybe he had something more but all the other players were important as well.

In my opinion if we had, had a player like Barmby in the squad perhaps with Juninho and myself , without being disrespectful to other players we could have been the best attack in the league . We played together the 3 of us in some very good matches against Everton and Liverpool for example, at the beginning of the season , we were doing very well in the league and Barmby was playing, we were very well positioned in the league it was a pleasant surprise for everybody, Barmby was scoring goals, I was scoring goals, Juninho was scoring goals, we were 3 complementary players and I don't know why he was sold.

BERNIE

I must ask you about your relationship with Mikkel Beck, did you get on throughout the game, you used to point the finger?

RAVANELLI

I was always trying to liven him up a bit, I was trying to help him understand, also in training the way we were trying to play together.

My gestures were not intended to blame him, he was a bit of a strange lad , very reserved, you just could not manage to understand what he was thinking. He had some good footballing skills, but he did not have a great personality on the pitch.

I have absolutely nothing against him, maybe if he had tried to understand me in a different way, for all the things I used to say to him were intended for his own good.

When playing he would only think about scoring a goal and that was not necessarily a good thing, of course it is an important thing for an attacking player to score especially for the self confidence, but a centre forward must primarily think about what is good for the team.

If I have the opportunity to pass the ball to a team mate for him to score then I do it, I pass the ball to him not being selfish, and if I'm not mistaken many of the goals he scored were from my assists so it is clear that I was trying to help him.

BERNIE

Who were you closest to at Boro?

RAVANELLI

One player I got on very well with was Gianluca Festa , he was an Italian like me, I also got on very well with Juninho, I had no particular problems with Steve Vickers, Robbie Mustoe, I had no problems whatsoever with most of the players.

There were some players who tried to make things up for me .I remember one time coming back from a match, playing in Naples in Italy for the national team. It was a very important qualifying match for the world cup against Poland, I had to come back to Middlesbrough the day after the match, the match was delayed and ended up late at night from Naples there were no flights available to come back till the next day.

I want to share this episode with you which will make people realize that jealousy was present in the dressing room. One player who's name I'm not going to tell, but if he was reading this interview will recognise himself said on the eve of the match against Aston villa a very important game that I did not behave like a professional for not returning straight back to Middlesbrough, he said that in the papers and I got very angry .

We won that match in which I scored 3 goals and took the responsibility to kick a penalty in injury time, a huge responsibility. Who knows what, maybe someone was jealous and wanted to cover for their own mistakes by putting the blame on me.

BERNIE

Where did the goal celebration come from, and would you do it if you had a big belly?

RAVANELLI

No if I had a beer belly , I would not.

I was playing in a match with Juventus against Napoli and the manager said to me at half time "calm down." The whole team was very nervous, the score was 0-0 and it looked like we couldn't score . Then he said to me that only some magic from a top class player would resolve the match. With 5 minutes remaining I scored a great goal, so his prediction was right, by instinct I lifted my shirt up and since then I've kept on doing it every time I score a goal.

BERNIE

You went on record as saying Middlesbrough's training facilities and methods were poor, what exactly did you mean?

RAVANELLI

Every criticism that was coming out of me was directed at trying to improve things, a constructive criticism .

I remember when I arrived in Middlesbrough from Juventus such a big club with top training and medical facilities, I had to drive to the riverside stadium, get changed , drive in my car to Tollesby , train in a meadow surrounded by houses, people walking their dogs asking for autographs, that was unacceptable, you can't fully concentrate in a situation like that.

All I wanted was people to understand that if you want to be successful you need to have top training and medical facilities.

Recently I saw a programme on Italian TV showing the new wonderful facilities at Rockcliffe Park, so I like to think that my criticism was justified and my words hit the target and contributed to the building of Rockcliffe Park.

BERNIE

Do you regret your comments about pollution on Teesside?

RAVANELLI

I never said such things . I only said that the town was different from say London or Rome . I was happily settled and felt at ease on Teesside, as I was living in a beautiful countryside village Hutton Rugby next door to Gordon McQueen , I was happy.

Middlesbrough is an industrial town and surely I wont tell a lie about the fact that there might be a little bit of pollution but in saying this I don't want to offend anyone, every town has its own history and culture which you have to respect I was very happy in Middlesbrough and I want to stress it now that I have a microphone in front of me, so that nobody can go and change or twist my words .

Every time I am interviewed my words are different now either I am insane which I am not, or there are individuals around who enjoy twisting my words.

There is also here the interpreter who I had at Middlesbrough and he can testify that for instance one time we did an interview, which turned out to be completely twisted and misinterpreted in the papers, where allegedly I had claimed that English players were all drunks, it was just a load of rubbish, I don't know maybe people in the English press did not like me and speculate by misquoting me as soon as they had the chance.

BERNIE

People respect you as a player and top goal scorer, but also as arrogant and ignorant, a bit of a big head, is that a fair assessment?

RAVANELLI

Maybe that is what people think of me in England surely in Italy and France people don't think I am like that at all .

I have never had a problem with the Italian or French press only in England I had a problem and I don't know the reason why .

I want to say it once again, I was happy in England at Boro. Yes I had some differences of which people know the reasons so I won't waste time explaining them. The only big regret I have is that I left not on very good terms with the fans, because I love the people of Teesside, I love boro supporters, and I would love one day to return to Middlesbrough and repay the debt that I've got with the fans, because in spite of the thirty one goals that I scored, I was bitterly sorry that we were relegated.

BERNIE.

You were part of the team beaten in 2 cup finals and relegated, what went wrong?

RAVANELLI

Lets say it as it is.

I don't mean any offence or disrespect, but the reason we lost the league cup lies entirely with Bryan Robson . He's a good person, but when your team are winning a cup final in the 119th minute with a chance of making history for Middlesbrough football club, you have to use your substitutes.

We had 3 substitutions to make , Emerson was limping, he should have taken him off. He did not and we did not win . He didn't know what he was doing at the end of the match. It was not important which player had to come off , we had the possibility to operate 3 changes and we did not make one . One change every 20 seconds , 3 changes the referee would have blown the whistle, the game was over.

BERNIE

You scored 31 goals in total was that more than you anticipated?

RAVANELLI

Yes more than I expected, I did not expect to score 31 goals with a team that eventually got relegated . I was at the peak of my career on very fine form, and I also had a player alongside like Juninho who helped me score goals.

BERNIE

Why did you leave Middlesbrough and did you leave on good terms?

RAVANELLI

I left because I wanted to play in the World Cup and by playing in the 1st division there was no chance for me . I left by telling the chairman and the manager that I wanted to remain a Boro player, by going on loan for a year and coming back to Middlesbrough after that .They did not want to, never mind.

BERNIE

Would you like to return to England one day as a player or manager?

RAVANELLI

Yes I would like to do both, maybe at Middlesbrough with Bryan Robson.

BERNIE

My thanks to Ravanelli for such a candid interview.

HONOURS.

FABRIZIO RAVANELLI.

PLAYING CAREER HISTORY

1986-1989	Perugia
1989	Avellino
1989-1990	Casertana
1990-1991	Avellino
1991-1992	Reggiana
1992-1996	Juventus
1996-1998	Middlesbrough
1998-2000	Marseille
2000-2001	SS Lazio
2001-2003	Derby County
2003	Dundee FC
2004-2005	Perugia

PLAYING HONOURS (winners)

Juventus
1996	Champions League
1993	UEFA Cup
1995	Italian SuperCup
1995	Serie A Champions
1995	Italian Cup

SS Lazio
2000	Serie A Champions
2000	Italian Cup

CAPS   22 Full caps for Italy

6 *My ambition was to be a journalist for the Sunday Times. I never saw it as a posh paper, I saw it is the one with the proper articles.* **9**

On what he wanted to be,
other than a musician.

Take 11

Chris Rea

Chris Rea was born in Middlesbrough on 3rd April 1951 and since the interview he has released another 6 albums, the latest being The Road To Hell And Back.

The first time I had ever heard of Chris Rea, was when I signed for Middlesbrough, back in 1984, I was living in Westwood Avenue at the time in digs and I used to pass a house with a giant sized Chris Rea poster. On the back of that, I went and bought one of his albums called Shamrock Diaries, instantly I was hooked, every weekend when I used to return to Glasgow on the train I used to listen to his music.

I met up with Chris in a Newcastle hotel. Chris was a lot smaller than I anticipated, fairly straight laced with a dry sense of humour, with his graveley voice still intact.

The young waiter who served us our morning coffee and croissants, as he arrived at the table, he nervously dropped the lot, coffee everywhere. On the back of it he turned and said ,"it's not everyday I serve two superstars." Quite clearly he must have thought I was someone else.

At the end of the interview, Chris followed me into the toilets and lifted his shirt, he told me that since his health problems he had to inject insulin every day.

I last saw Chris live in early 2008 at the Newcastle city hall, he was quite clearly in good health and vocally excellent, better than ever and his guitar playing was on a par with Jimmy Hendrix.

To meet a Boro lad who's world renowned for his musical talent was to me an absolute dream, and I continue to listen to his music.

BERNIE

Chris you were born and bred in Middlesbrough, and went to Sacred Heart school, what kind of upbringing did you have?

CHRIS

Er, very Irish Italian you know.

I was only 50 yards from school. It used to be called St Philomenias then, I don't know what happened to St Philomenias, but they changed the name of the church to Sacred Heart, so there was an awful lot of that in your life, and also with the Italian side of the family an awful lot of Italy, you know, lots of uncles with accordions, mandolins, er dreaming about this land far away, you know, that was sunny and warm called Italy.

BERNIE

Sacred heart school was right next to Ayresome Park, did you used to look through the window and see the Boro players?

CHRIS

Yeh, we used to try and get in, try and nick through, there used to be a hole in our school yard fence and we'd try and nick in, just to see the size of the place, when you were a young kid you know, it was quite awesome.

I mean Ayresome Park wasn't that big, but to us at that time it was bigger than Wembley you know.

BERNIE

You turned to music aged 19, what influenced you who were your idols?

CHRIS

It was when I first heard blues records.

Er there was I slide guitarist called Tom Patton, some people call him Tom Paton and he was supposed to be the man that you first ever heard on a blues slide guitar rift.

And when I heard that guy and apparently he came before Robert Johnstone, er it just blew me away you know, and the next day I just had to go and get an electric guitar.

It was quite late, I was 21, 22, before I started doing it seriously.

BERNIE

You must have played football as a youngster, your father told me that Mannion and Hardwick were his idols, did you have any idols?

CHRIS

Brian Clough, Edwin Holliday , Willie Fernie , Arthur Kay , Ronnie Waldock , Billy McNeil , Walker , er Taylor in goal and then Bob Appleby took over from Taylor, I could go on for ever, I've just rolled a team off for you there, er Ray Yeoman.

BERNIE

You allowed Lets Dance to be mixed by Bob Mortimer and the Middlesbrough team, what did you think of the version, you must have heard it?

CHRIS

Yeh, I helped Bob do it .

Err all I remember is the night that Bob tried to sing on it ,err its one of those instances that you never forget in your life, an you always wished you had a little video camera, cause he was absolutely hilarious that night.

The straighter he tried to do it the funnier it was you know.

BERNIE

I met your father Camillo, he owned Reas café, were you never tempted to go into the ice cream business ?

CHRIS

Er,yes I worked for my dad, err but it was the classic father son relationship, you know, he wanted it done his way and I had new ideas at the time. We have never got on so well since I left.

BERNIE

Where you a bit of a rebel in your younger days?

CHRIS

Er yeh , suppose you could say so, I think all young people are.

BERNIE

If you hadn't made it in the music business, what would you have done?

CHRIS

I wanted to be a journalist, that was my ambition, yeh my ambition was to be a journalist, for the Sunday Times.

BERNIE

The big posh paper ?

CHRIS

Well I never saw it as posh, I saw it as the one with the proper articles, you know.

BERNIE

In football its an advantage to have a left foot, you're left handed

CHRIS

I'm left footed as well

BERNIE

Are you, left footed as well .Is that a disadvantage in the music business?

CHRIS

Err it was when I began.

I couldn't find a left handed guitar, err in the end I had to teach myself to play right handed. I played left handed for 3 years and then I changed, which wasn't easy mind you some people might say he plays better like that, as well.

BERNIE

You have got a new album out called King Of The Beach, it sees you returning to your traditional roots, what can your fans expect from the album?

CHRIS

Err I hope they just like it.

You know I'm useless about talking about my own records, I mean I will just find things wrong with them.

I never play my own records at home, a lot of people are surprised, but I couldn't bear to hear my own things all day long, cause I would keep finding things that I would like to change.

You know like Enzo Ferrari once said when he was asked what was his favourite Ferrari and he said the next one .

I feel the same about my records, that's why promotion is so difficult for me, you know as soon as I have delivered an album, I start making the next one.

And I have to promote an album like now while I'm working on the next one, (he burps) pardon me.

Er I don't want to talk about King Of The Beach I want to talk about the new record, but this always happens your always 18 months ahead.

BERNIE

You have been a tremendous success through out Europe, yet in the UK in the early days you where on the peripheral, did that frustrate you at the time?

CHRIS

Not at all actually it meant for a good normal life, you know .

I think the easiest part of my career was the late 80s, where we were selling a million records in Europe, and no one knew who I was in England, except Middlesbrough, but err it was nice, it was easy I could go round, just not get hassled by anything, and then after road to hell it all changed.

BERNIE

Early on in your career ,a lot of your songs where inspired by your upbringing in Middlesbrough, Stainsby Girls, Steel River, where do you draw your inspiration from at this minute?

CHRIS

I get it from where I am, I mean like King Of The Beach was written in a very strange place.

I went for a holiday last Christmas, where there was absolutely nothing there, just this one hotel and there was a lot of people who then gave me the inspiration for the songs, who where at this place who where a bit bemused that they couldn't spend money, cause there was nothing there just wild beaches.

It was an island in the Turks called Ciacos in the Atlantic Ocean.

I loved it, but a lot of people didn't like it because it wasn't flashy cosmopolitan, and they had no where to wear their flashy Armani clothing and stuff like that you know .

I just sat there in my old shorts you know and a lot of the songs are about loosing materialism and being relaxed , you know kick off them shoes throw them away, enjoy the salty blue day.

BERNIE

You have tested the water in the movie business, have you enjoyed it and are you looking to do more?

CHRIS

Err I enjoyed doing the silly things with Michael Winner, err it was good fun.

I don't think I'd do it again, err I didn't have any ambition to be an actor.

I was originally brought in on the movie to do the music, and he was running out of time and he still hadn't found anyone to play it, in the end he gave me an offer I couldn't refuse and err I took it up. It was a good laugh but err no I didn't have any big ambition.

BERNIE

18 albums produced, 20 million copies sold, have you got a favourite, you must have a favourite?

CHRIS

No I don't, I don't listen to my records.

BERNIE

But when your doing them is there not one that you really think?

CHRIS

Well when I'm live one of the things that people say is a strong point about Chris Rea live is there is always a spin on the live version, because live 4 people that's worked together for 17 years now, we can do different versions, you know on the beach goes into a reggie version now when we do it live, and we always take it somewhere else, you know which makes it more interesting, but the records themselves I never listen to.

BERNIE

How big a kick do you get out of performing live, is that the icing on the cake?

CHRIS

You do your recording stuff in the studios, then like they are different things, you know writing and making and creating is just a compulsion. I've discovered over the years that there's a fine line between autism being an autistic and being a creative person, its definitely a compulsion, I have to do it 2 or 3 times a week, I have to write something otherwise I will feel as if there's something missing.

BERNIE

Do you enjoy the writing side?

CHRIS

Its more of a compulsion , something I have to do , like you have to comb your hair, have a shower, you have to write something. Err the live side is just the joy of playing with the band you know.

Err I mean Max Middleton is still my favourite piano player and I still count myself very lucky to go out to play for 2 hours a night with Max Middleton.

BERNIE

People always try and pigeon house musicians, saying they are rock, pop, or soul artists, where do you fit in, I believe in Ibiza you've got dance records out, where do you put yourself?

CHRIS

Er well I don't know, I'm really the good side of not being like anyone else, if you do you have a bit of longevity in your career which is what I've always wanted, you know I always said many years ago that I would rather have an album that goes to number 19 for the rest of my life, than 2 albums that go to number 1 and then no career, err cause it's the music that I like.

The downside of being your own man an individual is that sometimes your not in fashion and you have to accept that.

You know sometimes Chris Rea records sell while I'm in bed asleep, and sometimes no matter what you do they wont sell, and err you go to a country where a record is doing well, that's always happening with us, with 18 albums there will always be one country where its doing well and so we will go there, err I have no regrets.

BERNIE

You have not performed live for 2 years, why such a long break , or is it a long break.

CHRIS

2 years isn't long , and it wouldn't have been that long if I hadn't got ill. We had to cancel the tour in June, because they really didn't know what the outcome of the operation was going to be.

BERNIE

You have played in front of massive audiences around the world, never been tempted to play in front of your home crowd at the home of Middlesbrough Football Club , The Riverside?

CHRIS

No because I don't see myself as that type of artist you know.

I'm very popular in Middlesbrough, because I come from Middlesbrough, but I'm not the kind of artist that does stadium concerts, you know I'm not a big rock star, I don't have a rock star show, my life is about music, sound ,guitars, different types of guitars, different types of keyboards, a different type of music.

My life isn't about showbiz and err there is a big difference between showbiz and just been a musical person.

BERNIE

You have never been tempted even to play in the smaller venues of Middlesbrough?

CHRIS

That would be just, I just couldn't get away with it, it would be chaos.

BERNIE

Chris thanks very much for your time.

CHRIS

A pleasure.

HONOURS

CHRIS ANTON REA

SOLD OVER 30 MILLION ALBUMS

ALBUMS 24 in total:

1978	Whatever Happened To Benny Santini?
1979	Deltics
1980	Tennis
1982	Chris Rea
1983	Water Sign
1984	Wired to the Moon
1985	Shamrock Diaries
1985	Willie and The Poor Boys
1986	On The Beach
1987	Dancing With Strangers
1989	The Road To Hell
1991	Auberge
1992	God's Great Banana Skin
1993	Espresso Logic
1996	La Passione
1998	The Blue Café
1999	The Road To Hell: Part 2
2000	King of the Beach
2002	Dancing Down The Stony Road
2003	Blue Street (Five Guitars)
2003	Hofner Blue Notes
2004	The Blue Jukebox
2005	Blue Guitars
2008	The Return Of The Fabulous Hofner Blue Notes

‘ He *is one of the* *greatest guys I* *have ever met,* *and one of the* *best footballers,* *most certainly,* *the best* *footballer that I* *have signed and* *probably worked* *with,* *great talent.* **’**

Referring to Dennis Bergkamp.

Bruce Rioch

Bruce, despite being capped by Scotland, was born in Aldershot on September the 6th 1947, Bruce joined Middlesbrough in January 1986.

As a player he played for a host of clubs, he was a tough tackling, no nonsense wing half.

I met up with my former manager at the Royal County in County Durham.

After making sure I was immaculately dressed and clean shaven I was ready for the interview, as a player I was forever being fined for lacking both qualities.

Bruce was as enthusiastic as ever talking about the game of football. The one thing that I noticed about Bruce or Gadaffi as the players use to call him, was that he had mellowed, thank God.

I found him bright, sharp intelligent and intellectual the best communicator out of all my interviews.

BERNIE

Bruce you played for Luton, Derby, Everton and Aston Villa, why so many clubs?

BRUCE

Well I think they are certain reasons Bernie why people move in their career.

And in the period that I was playing, the reason that I moved from one club to another was purely ambition.

I began as a young 15 year old at Luton and served there from 1963 till 1969, and the club was still in the 3rd division at that stage and I just felt it was time to move on.

Actually I didn't ask to leave the club, I was quite happy at Luton. It was typical home town club, and one day the manager, Alex Stock came to see me on the training ground, pre season and just said, that they had accepted an offer from Aston Villa and that I had to meet Tommy Docherty and Arthur Cox was the coach then at Northampton.

Well I couldn't drive, didn't have a car, and they took me up to Northampton, and I met the manager who was Tommy Docherty and we agreed the deal.

The transfer deals in those days only took 5 minutes. Sat around the table they told me what they were offering, I said "great" and I went to villa, which was in the second division.

I knew their gates were in the region of 40,000, it was potentially a big club, so this was an ambitious move.

I had 5 years at Aston Villa, a great football club and I enjoyed it at Villa Park. But the 1st year we were relegated, into the 3rd and it took us one season to get back out.

And then after 5 seasons we were still in the 2nd division and I was getting to the age of 26, and I just felt I had to make a move into the old 1st division, to test my capabilities in that division before I finished my career in football.

I felt if I hadn't moved at that time at the age of 26, maybe a couple of years later I may have been too old to move. Err the management were superb Vick Crowe and Ron Weilly basically told me to continue playing, work hard and in the February of 74, I was again called off the training ground, and they told me they had accepted an offer from Derby County, who were one of the top clubs in that period.

I went along to meet the manager, who was Dave McRay another Scotsman, and I again signed immediately, so I was into the 1st division and Derby were third in the table at that time.

I joined and they hadn't won a game for 9 matches following the dismissal of Brian Clough in the October and err it was a big club, and a football town, a football city, and then after a couple of seasons, 2 and a half years possibly, Dave McRay lost his job and the first move I made without ambition was to Everton at that time they weren't any bigger necessarily than Derby County were, and I moved across to Everton, but I only stayed a year then I came back to Derby.

I really was unsettled at Everton, I was in an unsettled period of my life, err I had been very settled for all the previous years.

I spent 11 years at 2 clubs, 2 and a half years at Derby, then the unsettling effect of managers leaving, and we had a team that was capable of not only winning the championship, which we did do, but the following season we finished 4th, and the semi final of the cup. I actually might have won the double that year, very close to doing the double, and I felt that the change of manager was wrong.

I was now 29 years of age, the club accepted an offer from Everton and I thought well if you want to part company with me I will go, so I went, but then came back and spent another couple of seasons, so all those moves actually, the first 3 were purely ambition, there was no other reason for the moves.

BERNIE

You earned 24 national caps for Scotland, who were the opposition in your 1st game?

BRUCE

It was Portugal at Hampden Park and we won 1-0 and actually there is little story to my selection for the national team.

The season had ended Derby had a particularly good season, and as usual with some of the clubs we went away to Cala Millor in Spain, a place you know well. And err, we were there for just over a week, enjoying ourselves and relaxing at the end of a busy season.

We came back, I was at home and the telephone rang and it was the manager Dave McRay on the phone, and this is how the conversation went. "Hello Bruce how are you?" I said "fine," he said "how would you like to play for Scotland?" I said "oh I would love it." He said, "Well you have to ring a Mr Donald as in duck."

So I got on the phone to a Mr Donald in Scotland and he said, "How would you like to come and join us? We have got 5 games, a friendly match, the home internationals and erm a European championship game in Romania." So I said "great."

So I joined them up in Scotland, and to my surprise I was selected for the 1st game, because I thought well 5 games, if I get one game for Scotland that will be fantastic and I got picked for the 1st game against Portugal. And err it was a great match, we had Dalglish, Danny Mcgrain, Stuart Kennedy, Sandy Jardine, I think Eddie Gray may have played, Asa Hartford .

I mean it was just great; it was a great feeling to go to Hampden and get a win.

I got subbed after about 70 or 75 minutes the San-miguel pouring out of my calf's, at about 75 minutes and I thought, well great, I have enjoyed that.

I played in all of the other 4 games and I actually got my 1st goal against Wales, playing down at Wrexham. It was great and really fantastic and something that I had always wanted to do. And err the feeling of actually putting on the blue jersey and representing your country, is probably the best feeling you will ever get.

BERNIE

You played and captained Scotland in the 1978 World Cup Finals in Argentina, what went wrong? You lost to Peru, drew with Iran and beat Holland, who were a good side, the time Archie Gemmel scored a tremendous goal.

BRUCE

Well actually I don't blame anybody for it because, I thought it was a good experience, a tremendous learning experience

For those who came away from Argentina in 78, not having learnt from what took place would be fools, err under Willie Ormond if I could go back just a little bit under Willie the previous manager, he put together a team and a group of players, that were more like a club team . Every time we teamed up for our meetings and our matches it was invariably the same players, there might have been the odd occasion somebody else would come into the squad. But we actually got to know each others play so well.

Then he left and Ally Mcleod Came along and there was changes in the personnel and err the changes; in a way just disrupted the continuity of the team.

I don't think people do that on purpose, I think we all have our own ideas of who we would like to play in the team, and who we don't but it did disrupt, a little period before going away, it wasn't as harmonious as it should be in a team.

Where as in those early days, I think we had only lost something like 4 games in 20 internationals leading up to the world cup, and that was a pretty fantastic record.

And I think I ended up with 6 defeats in 24 games, something in that region, which is reasonable at international level.

But most certainly the changes and also there was a debate on money, and when you start having a debate on money and bonuses and your actually at the finals then nobody is going to win, and I think it kills morale and that took place.

The facilities weren't up to standard, so there were some areas that we look back on that weren't conjunctive to having a good environment for the team, but it was a good experience, I have to say that.

We failed to qualify to the next stage on goal difference, it wasn't points at all, and it was just a goal difference. So we were very close to getting through, and had we beaten Holland 3-1 as appose to 3-2, 3-1 we were through into the next round, so it was pretty close. But a good learning curve and something that you take with you in the long term when you go into management.

BERNIE

Was it always an ambition to become a manager, and who were your role models?

BRUCE

I think so.

For as long as I can remember, as a player especially living in the Midlands, and while I was with the Villa, I used to go to a lot of games.

I would go to Birmingham City midweek, I'd go to Derby, and I'd go to Coventry, West Brom and Wolves.

And I would ask my managers to obtain guestroom passes for me for half time, or before the game.

I used to go in and wait to talk to the managers, and I had the great opportunity to go in at West Brom one night, and meet Bill Shankly and Reuben Bennet.

This was the question I asked because I wanted to gain some information, I said to Bill Shankly. "Excuse me Mr Shankly can I ask you a question?" He stood there hands on his hips and said "what is it son?" I said "well when you buy players, obviously they have got to have talent and they have got to have ability, but is there something else your looking for?" And he said "yes son, they must play 42 games a season."

And I have never forgotten that.

I don't buy players who only play 20 games a season through injuries or suspension. And so going into those rooms and talking to those managers, was invaluable, you get coaching tips you get management tips and they have got to stay with you and register with you.

So I'd be 25 years of age maybe younger, going to theses games and spending my energy on evenings out watching football, which I loved and enjoyed, and I suppose that was the beginning for me.

BERNIE

You came to Boro as coach in 1986, under the manager Willie Madren, how did that come about?

BRUCE

Well I had gone back to Seattle in 85 to ...

BERNIE

You like Seattle don't you?

BRUCE

I love Seattle, I've been 3 years there it's a fantastic city, a great place to live. The North American soccer league as it stood had folded round about 84.

Some friends wanted to resurrect and keep football alive in America. And they asked me to go out and set up a league down on the west coast. So I went out along with people like Jimmy Gabriel and 1 or 2 others, and we set up a league which was comprised of, Vancouver, Victoria, Seattle, San Jose, Portland, Los Angeles, and San Fransisco.

And we set this league up and kept soccer running. And we had soccer camps and day camps and ladies teams and regional teams, it was a tremendous project, and it was important to keep the American scene running. I spent a year out there and erm basically the adrenalin stopped, because there was no real competition, as against having Manchester Utd play Liverpool the adrenalin flows, we didn't have the competition, so I came back in October or November that same year.

I was working as a scout for Arthur Cox at Derby, and err then I saw the application in one of the national papers for a coach to Middlesbrough.

I applied for it a had an interview, and before I had the interview I drove down to see Middlesbrough play Brighton, I think it was a 3-1, 3-3. You played in behind the front 2 and I went down to have a look.

I thought I'd better have a look at the team before I go to the interview.

Had the interview, Willie offered me the job on the Monday, and err that was really how I got the job at Middlesbrough football club in the first place.

BERNIE

A month after joining Willie was sacked, you became manager. Did that come as a surprise?

BRUCE

Well a little bit of background to Willie leaving.

I think I was going down to Portsmouth, err I think we lost down at Portsmouth.

And Willie had said to me on the way back, that he was under pressure and err he said "if I don't get the results, cause I love the club I might go."

And I persuaded him not to jump, not to walk out , not to resign, because it has been told to me in the past, Even though I was just in the beginning of management, that you didn't resign from jobs.

And then after one of the home games, he was sent for by the chairman Alf Duffield, well we were both sent for.

We went up to the manager's office, it might have been the secretary's office. David Thorn and err the chairman asked me to go next door, while they had a chat to Willie.

I was standing next door and 5 minutes after I thought, well to hell with this I'm not going to stand here and I went back down to the dressing room, and then another member of staff came up half an hour later and said the chairman would like to see me, Steve Smelt and Don Oriodon In the boardroom.

And he explained that Willie had left, and he said that he would like us 3 to look after the team.

I basically said "well with respect, I didn't see it proper that a player should be involved in the team," and I said "that I think that Don should leave the room." So Don left the room and he just asked me to take over and look after the team in the interim period, that's really what happened. The rest they say is history.

BERNIE

We were relegated that season was the job bigger than you anticipated?

BRUCE

No I didn't anticipate anything at all.

I came in with an open mind, to what had taken place at the club.

I wasn't fully aware of the finances at the club, when you're a coach you just concentrate on working with the players, you don't get involved in any of the financial side, and you leave that to the management and the board of directors.

Err and there was no money to spend and then we had a bad freeze period, where we didn't play for some time, and I think we went up to Scotland to play Celtic in a friendly match. And err it gave me a chance to get to know some of the players and we had a staff of about 30 odd players, and it gave me a chance to get to know some of the players better and then came the end of the season.

And again my position was not insularly that of a manager. I had no contract, although I was probably a caretaker at that time, but we had to make a decision on players and out of 34 or 5 players that we had on our books, I relegated 20.

BERNIE

I am glad to say I wasn't one of them.

BRUCE

You weren't one of them, no we held onto you.

And when we look back on the 14 or 15 that we kept in the short space of time that we had to work with the team, I don't think we made a mistake with any of them, not one .

We kept the right ones, and the only player who actually went on to do better things that we relegated was David Currie. He actually left Middlesbrough on a free and went on to Darlington, then from Darlington to Barnsley then Forrest. So he went on and did very well for himself, the rest basically fell by the wayside.

But there was some good lads there we didn't release them because they were all bad players.

There was different reasons err age, lack of desire, lack of drive, to young, to old,

good characters but not good enough ability. So there where different reasons as to why we released them.

The ones that we kept, we looked at these shirts we had but we didn't look at the number on these shirts we used to see a dollar sign on these shirts, and we looked at them and said do they have a market value, and we looked at them and said yes they do.

You might have played in a number 7 shirt, but we didn't look at it as a number 7 shirt. Did you have a market value? Yes you did in our opinion and did Peter Beagrie Have a market value? Yes he did.Mobray, Pallister, Cooper, Kernaghan, and Archie Stephens ? Yes, everyone had market value on their shirts, that's why we kept them. The others we felt didn't have a market value.

BERNIE

The club went into liquidation, the players received their wages from the town hall, where you paid at that particular time.

BRUCE

No no, none.

In fact, err we went into liquidation, I went off on holiday to Cala Milor. I was in the hotel with my wife and children, and the provisional Liquidator rang me and he said, "I have some news for you and its not necessarily good news, I'm afraid we are going to have to terminate your employment, or you can stay with the club and work for the club without wages." So I said in the reception of the hotel with a San-miguel in my hand, I was 3 days into my holiday of 14 days, and I thought to myself well hang on a minute, I may as well enjoy the rest of my holiday and I just said to him, "I will work for nothing."

I had nothing else to do except enjoy my holiday. He said fine. I went back downstairs carried on as normal enjoyed the rest of my holiday and came back, that's exactly what happened.

And just prior to going on holiday I had a call from Steve Smelt the physio, to say he was leaving to go to Sunderland, and Danny Begara Rang me to say he was leaving to go to Sheffield, so we had lost the staff as well, but I couldn't blame them for leaving, cause there was no guarantees.

And Toddy, who I had taken out of a job working for Vaux breweries to join us just prior to that, he wondered what the hell was happening as well, so he was out of work as well basically.

None of us were getting wages. And the worst part of it all really was for Toddy and Barry Geldart, driving you lot to the town hall and having to confirm that you were all players and having to sign you all in for your wages. Because they saw you all picking up money and they were to pick up no wages at all.

But at that time I paid the lodging money to the land lady of all the yts lads.

BERNIE

Out of your own pocket?

BRUCE

Yes and I paid the wages of the kit manager and repairs to cars, there was a lot I did financially, which eventually I got back from the club, when the club resolved itself, but I didn't know whether it was going to happen or not. I just felt it was important to keep the same people on board.

It was important to keep the land ladies incomes going into them and the yts wages going in and so forth.

And to be fair to the club they did reimburse me, err when everything was settled eventually.

Some of the things that happened to the players were wrong, and for those players who wanted to move on, so be it, but without the players who stayed there wouldn't have been a Middlesbrough football club as we know it today.

The home grown players and yourself and er Archie Stephens, they stayed they continued to support each other and work for the club, cause the club was their love. And it wouldn't be the Middlesbrough FC as we know it today had they all decided to get up and move, there wouldn't have been a professional team we would have had to start in the conference league or some where else so Middlesbrough is here because of the players.

BERNIE

So what do you remember about the liquidation scenario?

BRUCE

Oh there are so many stories, oh dear I think the worst one was the radio.

One of the kids coming in and saying well we have heard on the radio we are going bust today, and I can remember saying to the group on several occasions, until you here it from me, we are surviving, and we are going on , you just concentrate on your training and err we are going on.

I remember one day at Longlands College when we were training in the college and I wasn't happy with the way training was going, I think it was on a Thursday and I called all the players together, and of course you lads were getting paid and Toddy and I weren't.

And I said "look we are not here to muck about," and I said this that and the other, "as far as we are concerned you make your minds up. We are going home for the weekend and you can do what you want and we will see you Monday."

And I think you all got together and went into the local park and trained together. And I think those sort of things brought you all back together, tighter. But it started off in the boardroom with a deficit of about 80,000, and a million, and 1.2 ,and 1.6 and it seamed to be going up, every time you opened a cupboard a skeleton fell out and the money went up.

But I had made a conscious decision that I wasn't going to get involved in any way, shape or form with regard to the finance of the club.

My whole and total effort was going to be focussing on the team and it was probably the best period of my life, for working with players.

I didn't have to worry about buying players, or doing any homework or office work. I just focussed on the team and worked with the team to get a spirit and that in itself was great .

And that experience that I raised earlier in the conversation with regards to Torquay was the experience that has lasted me for the future.

And I remember changing in the, I don't know what you would call it err the equipment room at Longlands, you chaps changed in the dressing room and Toddy and I changed in the top end of the cupboard.

And Toddy was saying "bloody hell this is diabolical"

And I said "Toddy I had it worse at Torquay."

And so every day we'd start, we were the brightest guys that you have ever met, although we might moan and groan in behind the scenes when we faced the boys ,we feel great, were brilliant, were fantastic, were up beat every day.

We preached it because we felt if the players saw us down and low, then it might transmit itself on to one or two and we wouldn't allow that.

And actually I carried that through all of my career in management, so it was a good sign, a lot of good days, actually it brings back a lot of good memories.

BERNIE

Did you always have faith that the club would be saved?

BRUCE

Yes I did because historically other clubs that had being relegated or going out of business, or out of the league everyone survives. And err there has been 1or 2 other clubs in difficulty.

I believe that there is always some one who is going to come along and help a club, it's a big football club Middlesbrough, they have great traditions and one of my if not my all time favourite was, Wilf Mannion.

I was living in Cambridge, when Wilf came at the end of his career and played at Cambridge Utd, so here I am at a club where one of my hero's played. I couldn't see it going under.

I mean they had great tradition, err we had good players, good group of young players, and Steve Gibson who was young, is still young now, but 27 or 28 at the time. He was a go getter, he was hard nosed, determined to take the bull by the horns and go forward, I couldn't see it going under .

And so as I said, I just focussed my whole attention onto the players, and making sure that they were prepared and ready for the start of the season, which they were.

BERNIE

In your first full season in charge you gained promotion from the 3rd to the 2nd, did that amaze You in any way?

BRUCE

Well I really didn't know what to expect, from the first season because we only had 14 players.

I think we went into that season with 14 players 15 at the most and err we knew we had some good young players, and we knew they had to grow up quite quickly.

And eer it was at that stage that a firm hand was necessary, there was a lot of young players 17 or 18 and 19 years old, I think the average age of the team was 20 years and a few months, when we went out to play against Port Vale at Hartlepool and I felt a firm hand, but a correct hand, would be right with the players, because it was going to be such an important period for them and the club.

And err we got off to a good start, and if you remember we went to Wigan early on and we got battered in the first half at Wigan.

And I can remember going up the tunnel at half time and their left back saying, they are hopeless. And I can remember coming into you lot at half time and saying look their left back has just said we are hopeless and they had thrown everything at us, bar the kitchen sink and they still can't score.

And we went out and I think we won 2-0, and that was a run of about 12 or 13 games undefeated we were on at the beginning of the season.

BERNIE

At the beginning of the season you used to actually set targets didn't you?

BRUCE

Yes I did, I still do .

For the club and for the players and I set targets for goals for the players, and targets for clean sheets. Its motivation for them it gives them something to hang onto.

BERNIE

So what would a target for a midfielder be?

BRUCE

Well we would say for the midfielder's 40 goals, 10 a piece, give us 40 goals across the midfield.

Not necessarily possible, but you might have one midfielder, who might get 18 goals in a season, cause that's his capabilities and someone else might get 9. Some body else might get 6, but give them a target that they might attain.

Err and the strikers we used to say 20 goals a piece or 25 a piece, 20 a piece is 40 goals. 40 from midfield is 80 you've got a championship team there and if you get 4 or 5 from your back line.

So it was good to set targets and I think that 1st season, I think we had such a strong bond as a group in that first period, err that is because there was so few of us, an everybody was so friendly and warm with each other they really were, err I think it was fantastic.

I remember one day on the training ground with yourselves in liquidation and in difficult times for us all. When at Hutton road you and Pearsy had a very inopportune incident, but Pearsy butted you and I sent him off the field, and you started to argue, and I said "don't argue you're in enough trouble already, so get back to the ground," and he went back and we finished the training session and we all went back and I sent for him .

And he came up the corridor into the referee's room at Ayresome Park, he walked in and I said to him "are you ok?" He said "Yes." "Now go down and shake your pals hand and say your sorry." And he came down to the dressing room, walked in and said sorry to you and that was the end of it. But it was difficult for you lads as well, it was difficult for all of us.

I thought we all came through those days so well together. It was phenomenal, some of the greatest memories, forget the downsides, cause there is always, going to be downsides in some peoples lives, when you think of all the plus sides in that era in that period, then you can cast your memories back on, and all the chaps will, and I will, oh phenomenal, a great moment in our lives.

BERNIE

The following season you gained promotion to division one via the playoffs against Bradford and Chelsea, did you honestly believe that a group of local talent could make it into the top flight?

BRUCE

Well having got up the first year we added a couple of players.

I think we had £ 30,000 to spend on Paul Kerr during the first season (nookie bear), could play any where and everywhere. Err and then we had a little more money to spend and we bought Deano (spam head), remember spam head, and Deano could play centre back and he could play midfield, he played a lot of games in midfield for us in that period.

And we bought Sprouty, he came along as back up goalie, err so we had 3 young players at the right age integrated into the club, which I felt integrated very well. And they were all from the same club all from Aston Villa.

I went to Aston Villa and looked at them and scouted their training ground and watched the training and picked 3 youngsters out of their team at the right price, and they integrated very well.

Err but I didn't feel that we were going to get up that season. I just thought that we were going to have a good year, cause we have got another years experience and we were going to have a good season with the boys. And we went all the way to the play offs.

And in fact on the very last day of the season we were playing Leicester at home and looking back I made an error.

The error was I didn't take the boys away on the Friday night. As you know we are at this moment at the Royal County in Durham.

In the initial period of being together, we came here every Friday night as a a team and had dinner in a private room.

We had our birthday parties in private rooms, we had the cakes remember that, it was all part of building team spirit. And erm as the team grew older and had girlfriends or wives, one or two came forward and said could we forfeit the Friday nights away for the home matches and we did that.

But that was an occasion when with so much tension and excitement we should have taken the team away on the Friday night.

Because the club started gearing itself for a carnival and a festival, which I didn't like it was done behind the scenes, and you know just come and bring all your flags and roar the team on into the 1st division.

And I thought it is not as easy as that, this game you never take for granted, and err the players were turning up at 1- o- clock for a 3- o- clock game, well that was unusual.

And it was a very hot day and we lost 2-1.

And so for the playoffs we took you all away into a hotel for the 2nd legs of the games. And particularly for the Bradford City game, took you into a hotel for the home and away Bradford city games, so that we were all together, so that we could all share the tension if there was going to be any.

But really when you are all together you actually don't feel the tension so much you bounce it off each other. And err we realised we may have done it automatically, had we done it that way round.

And err I can remember coming up after the loss against Leicester, during the press conference, you know how the dressing room was, and coming back down and actually giving you all a speech as a group for about 15 to 20 minutes, of how we were going to do it, and what we were going to do, and we hadn't come this far without succeeding and this, that and the other and err yeh we did it.

BERNIE

We entertained in the top flight and earned rave reviews for the way we played, but we couldn't avoid relegation why?

BRUCE

Well again if you look at it realistically.

We came from 3rd division to 1st in 2 seasons and at the time the club was in liquidation, debts of 1 and a half to, 2 million, well just call it 2 million, debts of 2 million, a squad of 14 players to start the 3rd division, added 1 or 2 more along the way, a squad of 16 or 17 players maximum going into the 1st division, you can't survive on that.

And then we picked up 1 or 2 injuries along the way and when we went past transfer deadline day and we couldn't purchase anyone else, or loan anyone else, any injuries after that period and there was a few, we couldn't replace.

And I can remember going to the last game of the season at Sheff Wed and we took all the lads with us, and you will remember we took all the injured into the dressing room before the game.

And there was maybe 3 or 4 players on crutches unable to play. And we were actually calling on you young pros, young yts, to be back up or even in the team itself.

Some players like Gary Hamilton played with bad injuries on that particular day. We just didn't have enough strength and back up strength, we just were too soon and too quick, and we didn't have enough resourses and players coming that way so fast, to build the team and increase the teams strength.

And err obviously you would like to have gone quicker or once you go into the 1st division as we were and come out, some who've tasted it want to leave.

BERNIE

The following season you guided Middlesbrough to their 1st ever Wembley appearance in their history, but before we got to the final you were sacked, did you feel angry let down betrayed?

BRUCE

No I don't use those words err at all.

Disappointment yes, err because we had had a poor league season but our cup prospects were excellent.

I think we had beaten Sheff Wed in a quarter final and played exceptionally well.

We played Villa over 2 legs and tactically as you will look back and say, tactically we played a different way at Villa Park. I think we played you on the left wing at Villa Park and Alan Kernaghan up the middle but we did it for a reason. We played Alan Kernaghan and Stuart Ripley up the middle to run the legs off McGrath At the back, which we did, err I think we won 2-1.

I think Mark Brennan Scored a free kick.

And then we came back home and we put you up the middle.

I think they scored 1st and then you scored, what I described as probably one of the finest goalscorers goals you will ever see, quick, feet shuffling from right to left, put it right in the roof of the net, inside the postage stamp of the left hand post.

And err you know that was a great night. I think we were the only team that did the double over Villa.

And our tactics were right because they had the runners in Daley and Platt and they had the passers in Gordon Cowans

And we put Mark Proctor on the passer Gordon Cowans A man marking job and the idea was if you stop the supply, then the runners can run all day and they are not a problem, and that's really what happened.

And tactically we got it right and there was the 1st cup final in the clubs history. And then I think it was about a week to 10 days before I lost my job.

In fact here we are in March 1999, its 9 years almost to the day.

On the day that Middlesbrough played at Wembley March 1990, Jane and I went for a walk around as we did regularly.

We went for a walk around Durham Cathedral and actually I went and sat in the Cathedral tonight before I came here. I went into the Cathedral just after 5-o-clock and I was in there for the service until 6-o-clock before coming to see you.

So it brought back all those memories, sad memories, but as I mentioned earlier to you Bernie, when you look at the up sides and the down sides.

The up sides were far greater and I tend to look at those rather than the down sides.

And I have no bitterness towards the club whatsoever now..

BERNIE

In 1995 you joined the mighty Arsenal, and signed several top players, including Dennis Bergkamp, how did you enjoy your time at Highbury?

BRUCE

Brilliant, great football club, one of the best in the world, a pleasure to have been there.

Err and I knew a bit about Arsenal because I had been brought up in the south, so I had been to see them play in the 60's and 70's.

And err traditionally they are awesome.

The opportunity to go there was just fantastic.

And I had the opportunity to spend some money on players, that I hadn't had else where. And the player that I bought was Dennis Bergkamp.

BERNIE

How much for?

BRUCE

I didn't negotiate those deals.

It was taken out of my hands, by the powers that be at the top end that's fine, but I think they paid about 7 million for him.

And it wasn't even a risk I mean sometimes you pay 30,000 for a player if you're at Torquay or Rochdale it could be a risk.

7 million for Dennis was a snip, he's a fantastic man, a wonderful guy.

Err I have never heard him complain, he's never missed a press conference, never missed a press interview, err a terrific family man, 2 children.

And err when I met him we talked about football for an hour non stop.

They said he was too serious a guy, when he came across there was question marks about the signing. He is one of the greatest guys I've ever met.

And one of the best footballers, most certainly the best footballer, that I have signed and err probably worked with. Great talent, great technique, trained hard, practices hard, just a wonderful guy, and a real team man. Loves England, loves English football, he hadn't come across here to make a quick buck, loves the football .

And err Arsenal a great football club Bernie, you have got to be there to understand what the Arsenals about.

BERNIE

Why did you only last one year?

BRUCE

I think there was a combination of reasons.

I fell out with Wrighty, he had a disagreement with another striker and I wanted to sell him, I didn't think we would win the championship with Ian Wright in the team that was my opinion.

And I wanted to sell him and get the best deal I could at the time.

We thought we might get 5 million for him if we sold him at the right time, I wanted to buy Shearer and I thought Shearer might cost, us 10 to 20 million, so if we bought and sold, that would be about 7 million transaction.

That was discussed in the boardroom and it came out of the boardroom and was made public, and they breached the confidence in there and that caused a problem.

He came to see me and said "I hear you want to sell me" and this that and the other, and we had a bit of a head to head at some stage. He argued for a transfer and it was denied and so on.

But I wanted to bring Shearer in and I had already bid at that time for Overmars

At that time he actually had a leg injury. Err we bid for Ron Deboer I wanted him in from Holland, I wanted the best players in, I was at one of the best clubs in the world, I wanted to have the best players. I felt that they had the resources.

I didn't sign a contract with them, because what we had agreed initially wasn't put on paper, I agreed, we agreed but it wasn't actually put on contract the way I had agreed it, so I wouldn't sign it, until it was amended, that got picked up by the media.

That added onto the dispute with Ian Wright etc, etc and eer Arséne Wenger who is a lovely man a very successful man, he was always the first choice for the club.

Even when I was there, I knew previously they had tried to get him from Monaco, but he had gone off to a Japanese club and he was way too long on contract when they took myself on, so they were waiting for him to become available.

Despite finishing 3rd and qualifying for Europe in the 1st year, a week before the season started I lost the job, and that was a real blow.

I mean you work your socks off in your life to get a job like Arsenal and you don't want to lose it lightly.

And err that was probably the biggest disappointment in my life.

BERNIE

In the future would you love to one day return to Middlesbrough and manage them or manage Scotland?

BRUCE

Oh I wouldn't say no to anything, because sometimes they say never go back, never return, but people do return and become successful at some clubs.

There's Toshack been at Real Madrid once and lost his job, and has now gone back again for a 2nd spell, err Howard Kendall at Everton went back again.

Err it depends on when you go back to a club, how the club is based, the circumstances of the club, are they in a good position is it a solid position.

Err invariably you get jobs when things aren't going well. But I have got a great deal of respect for Middlesbrough and the people, err it's the players and the supporters and Steve Gibson and his consortium that kept Middlesbrough Football Club alive, and it was a great football club and I enjoyed it, I don't have any ill feeling as I mentioned before to the club.

Only good memories really good memories, great stories.

I could relate so many stories here today ,that would be so humorous and successful times, in many respects , err if the opportunity was around the corner and it was right and it was proper and it suited everybody, well why not.

HONOURS

BRUCE DAVID RIOCH

PLAYING CAREER HISTORY

1964-1969	Luton Town
1969-1974	Aston Villa
1974-1976	Derby County
1976-1977	Everton
1977-1979	Derby County
1978	Birmingham City
1979	Sheffield United
1979-1980	Seattle Sounders
1980-1984	Torquay United
1975-1978	Scotland

MANAGERIAL CAREER HISTORY

1982-1984	Torquay United
1985	F.C. Seattle
1986-1990	Middlesbrough
1990-1992	Millwall
1992-1995	Bolton Wanders
1995-1996	Arsenal
1998-2000	Norwich City
2000-2001	Wigan Athletic
2005-2007	OB
2008	AaB

PLAYING HONOURS (winners)
Derby County

1974	League Championship

CAPS	24 Full caps for Scotland

**‘ To go to a club
like united, and
the expectations
were so
high about
winning the
Championship,
and err then
being the record
player, you
know, I found
that difficult in
the first period. ’**

On signing for Man. Utd.

Take 13

Bryan Robson

Robbo was born in Witton Gilbert on the 11th January 1957. He arrived on Teesside as Middlesbrough manager in the 1994/95 season, after 13 glorious seasons at Old Trafford.

As a player he was arguably one of the best midfielders in the world. He had fantastic energy levels, he could tackle, pass and drive forward, and score goals, he was an out an out leader.

I met with Robbo at Hartlepool Marina, amazingly the interview took place on a sailing boat, it was cold, windy and if I'm honest, uncomfortable, and you will never believe who was captain of the boat, none other than Bob Moncur the ex Newcastle United captain who had lifted the Fairs Cup back in 1969.

I had met Robbo plenty of times before this interview and had played in several charity games alongside him.

I have always found Robbo to be approachable and on this occasion it was no different, at one point myself and Robbo were pulling the masts to steer the boat clear of the harbour walls.

I had always being an admirer of Bryan as a player but during his time as manager of Middlesbrough in his opening 4 years the football was breathtaking, since his departure we have yet to recreate that standard.

BERNIE.

Bryan you started your career at West Brom in 1974, where you spent 7 years clocking up 194 games and scoring 39 goals, would you class them as 7 good years?

BRYAN.

Yes they were, I really enjoyed it at the Brom, cause there was some good managers there, Ron Atkinson was there.

BERNIE.

How did you get on with big Ron?

BRYAN.

I got on fine with Ron, right from the time when I'd played in quite a few games, and then he left me out of the semi final and we got beat against Ipswich down at Highbury, so I was a bit disappointed with him when he left me out of that one.

BERNIE.

How big a jump was it going to Old Trafford?

BRYAN.

Well the biggest jump for me at the time was the fee of 1 and a half million, and everyone was saying you're the record buy, and so from coming through from an apprentice and costing nothing, there was no expectations on you, to go to a club like United and the expectations where so high about winning the championship, and err then being a record player you know I found that difficult in the 1st period.

BERNIE.

You played in World Cups, big games for Man utd. My old mate Pally says that the 1991 cup winner's cup final against Barcelona in Rotterdam ranks as the best experience he's ever had in football. Where would you rank it?

BRYAN.

Yeh that was my best one I agree with Pally there. It was just European Competition, you know playing against Barcelona who had a fantastic reputation, and they had some world class players in Laudrop and Koeman. I think they were 3- 1 on with the bookies to win and the team had just come together, you had Pally who was fairly young at the time errr Paul Ince had come in Brian McClair and they were all just coming through, Alex Ferguson was just starting to build his team.

BERNIE.

What did you actually win in your 12 years at Old Trafford?

BRYAN.

Err I'm not sure how many charity shields it was.

BERNIE.

Oh they don't count surely.

BRYAN.

Err 4 FA Cups a European Cup Winners Cup, err we won the Super Cup and the 2 championships.

BERNIE.

Not bad is it.

BRYAN.

No it was pleasing, to finish off with the 2 championships towards the end, it would have been disappointing to go through my career without winning one of those.

BERNIE.

You played in all the major games for Man Utd, except the FA Cup final in the 95 season, Alex Ferguson decided to leave you out. How big a blow was that and how did you react?

BRYAN.

It was a big disappointment, my contract was coming up to its end, I had already spoken to Wolverhampton Wanderes about a job before err Middlesbrough had already approached me and I had spoke to Middlesbrough about the job, and I had an inclination that Alex Ferguson wouldn't involve me in the cup final.

But the thing that was really disappointing for me was I had played in all the earlier rounds in the semi final we were struggling in the first game and they brought me on as a substitute and we got back into the game and we drew the game err and that was when we had quite a few suspensions and I think it was Eric Cantona and Andrea Kanchelskis Missed the first game because of suspension and err yes in the replay Alex recalled Eric and Andrea. He recalled me into the team as well and we won the game 4-0 at Maine Road and so when your part of it and I scored a goal as well in the game I thought Andrea

Kanchelskis on the evening was the best player, but then I thought I was probably our 2nd best player on the night. So when you feel you have been part of the Semi Final like that, you feel you deserve at least a place on the bench in the Final.

BERNIE.

You became England coach under Terry Venables, how did that come about?

BRYAN.

Err it was a surprise really.

Terry Venables phoned me at the club and he just said "You fancy been involved with the England set up." He was going to take Don Howe on and he wanted me to work alongside Don and himself. So I had a think about it and I thought well its going to be a great experience, and I really enjoyed that job because all the pressure was on Terry as the manager and it was a sort of relaxing type of job err been involved with the England job to where I was but it was great working with the international players and I really enjoyed the Euro 96 yeh.

BERNIE.

Who would you say has been the best manager you have played under or is that an unfair question?

BRYAN.

Its an unfair question, because I think I've worked under a lot of tremendous managers who've had success in their own way, even at international level, I mean Ron Greenwood was a very good manager, Bobby Robson was a tremendous manager err club level Ron Atkinson had his success Alex Ferguson had his success. So what I have done is I have been able to learn a lot from these managers and hopefully it will make me a better manager in the long term.

BERNIE.

You joined Middlesbrough as player manager in 1994 season, how did that move come about?

BRYAN.

It was after a league game at Old Trafford , Alex Ferguson called me into his office and he said to me that there is a interest from Middlesbrough, and that

Lennie Lawrence would like to have a chat with me, and so I said "yes I would speak to him", cause I knew that I was going to move on from Utd at the end of the season, and so Lennie came in and he said that Steve Gibson and Keith Lamb had spoke to him and they would like his input as to who he feels could be the manager of the club.

BERNIE.

Did you feel at the time you had been thrown in at the deep end, no managerial experience just chucked right in there?

BRYAN.

No not really cause I'd seen certain players go from a player, to a player manager, and Alex Ferguson was really good to me over the last year and a half to two years. I used to drop the kids off at school, early in the morning and I used to go in, I was more or less first in every morning as far as the players were concerned and err he was very good cause he allowed me to go into the coaching room and so I saw the coaches setting up the days training and Alex used to let me sit in on the conversations they were having and that was a good experience for me.

BERNIE.

Was it always an ambition to be a manager?

BRYAN.

Yeh it was as a soon as I got to my mid 30's, I always had it in my mind that I would like to give it a crack.

BERNIE.

You've played the 5-3-2- formation for several years why?

BRYAN.

Sometimes you have got to go with what suits your players, and who you can buy at the time, and there's times when I've gone out and tried to buy quality wide players and if you're going to play 4-4-2 and be successful, you're going to need quality wide players, they just haven't been available or we have not been able to get them and so to me that's a big part of the 4-4-2 trying to find the Giggsy and the Overmars Of the world is very difficult.

BERNIE.

Your big name has attracted big name players, but they all disappeared within 2 years, how disappointing is that for you as a manager?

BRYAN.

Well its frustrating in a sense that if we hadn't got relegated then we would probably still be looking we'd have Emerson, Juninho and Ravanelli now if I had added people like Pallister, Cooper, Gordon to that squad with those type of attacking players we would have been a real side, but because of those players wanting to go, its had to be a bit of a rebuild err and you know we have had to take 2 steps backwards to go 3 steps forward again. So relegation was a blow, but it could have been a far bigger blow if we hadn't got promoted straight away again.

BERNIE

On the subject of big names, while they were here, there is no doubt they entertained, they were superb, but I've said this season on the radio that its not been the most entertaining season was this season about entertainment or consolidation, do you think we have entertained?

BRYAN.

I think we have entertained in certain games err but I wanted to have a good solid base with the British lads where I could get real good team spirit within the club, a good solid base of experience where we weren't going to get relegated err and I think we've achieved that now. The chairman is talking about giving me more money again, so this time I think that the structure of the club, as a club is tremendous now far superior to 2 years ago the basis of the squad of players is a lot stronger, not just as players but mentally, the way the lads approach the game and the characters of them and to me now that's given us a great platform now to try and buy 3 or 4 top players in the summer and to go on and try and better what we have done this season. There are a few players I have tried to sign as the seasons gone on and they just have not been available and the clubs wont sell them and its like say, if we are going to finish in the top 10 or even higher, to buy players they have to be better than the players that you have got now, if our lads have achieved say 8th in the league this season if we do finish that high I've got to buy us players who can get us higher than that and that's not an easy task because a lot of the good young players are with the likes of United and Arsenal and they don't want to leave, so you can never get any of them. Err if really good young British players become available and those clubs come in for them and you can hardly compete because the young lads want to go to them, cause they are winning things every year, that makes it difficult so you have got to go looking abroad again, you have just got to broaden your vision really and just have a look and see what you think is quality and what you can add to your squad to make a better team for the following season.

HONOURS

BRYAN ROBSON

PLAYING CAREER HISTORY

1975-1981	West Bromwich Albion
1981-1994	Manchester United
1994	Middlesbrough (player/manager)
1980-1990	England

MANAGERIAL CAREER HISTORY

1994-2001	Middlesbrough
2003-2004	Bradford
2004- 2006	West Bromwich Albion
2007-2008	Sheffield United

PLAYING HONOURS (winners)

Manchester United

1983	FA Cup
1985	FA Cup
1990	FA Cup
1991	Cup Winners Cup
1993	Premier League Title
1994	Premier League Title
1994	FA Cup

MANAGERIAL HONOURS (winners)

Middlesbrough

1995	Division 1 Title

CAPS	90 Full caps for England

'The biggest concern I had leaving Boro wasn't leaving Middlesbrough Football Club, it was leaving my landlady Feebie Haig.'

On him leaving Boro.

Take 14

Graeme Souness

Graeme was born in Edinburgh on 6th may 1953. Aged 16 he signed apprentice forms for spurs. In December 1972 after failing to command a 1st team spot he signed for Middlesbrough for a fee of £ 32,000. Souness was a skilful silky player, but was armoured with aggression and toughness.

I met up with Sou at his home. It was a scorching day and I did the interview next to a stream, before we got underway Graeme fed his pet coy carp.

I personally respected Souness obviously for every thing he did as a player and a manager, but to change a 100 year tradition in Glasgow while with Rangers took some balls. The gers as they are known have never signed a catholic footballer in their history Souness changed all that.

Sou was everything I expected straight, confident, laced with a hint of arrogance, it was quite clear by his luxurious surroundings, that he had been highly successful in his career both as a player and manager

BERNIE.

When you left school, you moved south, joining Spurs, why did you move south?

GRAEME.

Well I played for Scottish schoolboys, and we played England at White Hart Lane, and Dave Mackay had broken his leg, for the second time and errm he was watching the game. Well I went to the same school as Dave Mackay Bernie so he obviously took up more of an interest And I must have done alright, and after the game he recommended me, to Bill Nicholson, who invited me down there and at that time Tottenham were a big team, they were one of the best teams around.

I fancied getting out of Scotland, I trained at that time 15 I was training with

Celtic, who had there best team, they had just won the European Cup and I'd gone through to Ibrox to talk to Dave White, with the possibility of joining Glasgow Rangers, and I had a couple of other offers from teams in England. But I don't know I think from the first minute I went to White Hart Lane, I had my heart set on going there, I was delighted when they showed an interest.

BERNIE.

Things didn't quite work out at White Hart Lane, what attracted you to Teesside?

GRAEME

I was 19 and I was telling Bill Nicholson, I should be in the team. At the time there was Martin Peters, Alan Mullery and Steve Perryman in the midfield for Tottenham. From 17 onwards I was telling Bill Nicholson every Friday why was my name not on the team sheet, I should be in the team. Then in the end he just got cheesed off with me, he could have sold me I believe to Oxford was one of the teams and Millwall, and err he told me later that he had wanted to sell me as far away from London as possible, and err I just wanted to play 1st team football, and I have to admit there was no real attraction to Middlesbrough at that time, obviously when I got there I realised what a good place it was, how the people were, and how much in the end I really enjoyed it there.

BERNIE.

How was your relationship with big Jack Charlton, I believe Jack questioned your attitude.

GRAEME.

I think like a lot of youngsters, maybe I had too much too soon, you know I had played for the Scottish schoolboys, I had gone to Tottenham, who were a big glamorous club, I lived in London and at 19 going to Middlesbrough, I think he quite correctly, not think, I know he quite correctly hit me on the head, more than once, and reminded me what professional football was all about.

Simple things like you don't just play when you have the ball, you are a team member, and of course how you lead your life away from football, and I think in all those areas he helped me, not so much helped you, he just told you black and white it's this way or its Jacks way. If you wanted to stay there and be part of what he was doing it was Jacks way. I had no problem with that, I think Jack liked me, I think once I buckled down and worked hard, I think err we had a good relationship.

But in the early days he did hammer me, I'm saying early on he hammered me all the time, how can I put it, in a way you would your son. I had a good relationship with him; I had great admiration for him, because obviously that was a very important time in my development.

BERNIE.

The 1973/74 season was one of Boro's top seasons, what were the highlights?

GRAEME.

There was great times cause obviously I was only young, and the players there were all great mates and we got on famously. In any team your not going to get 15 or 16 guys that all love each other, but we were certainly together as a unit when it mattered, it was a smashing time to be there, it was just all happening .Jack was attracting enormous attention from the national media, it wasn't just localised in the north east, he was a big name throughout England, and we got a lot of media attention, and I think me included we all benefited from it, from Jacks fame, it was a good time to be at Middlesbrough and the supporters were seeing something new, they were seeing a Middlesbrough team that were going out and winning nearly all the games they played in and they enjoyed that as well, it was a good time to be around, it was a good time to play for Middlesbrough.

BERNIE.

Where you a natural or did you have to work at it?

GRAEME.

If I say I was a natural that sounds big headed. You're born with certain things, but I think I was fortunate, I was the youngest of 3 brothers, and our house was a prefab and it backed onto a school field, so every night I was out with my brothers playing football, and of course I was playing with people a lot older than me all the time so I think that dragged me on a lot quicker.

I would like to think I had a natural gift and err I think that the most pleasing part and I don't think that there's many players that can say that, but I actually feel I'd done as much as I could have done, with what I'd been given, I feel I had looked after myself after the Jack influence, after maybe going to Liverpool and learning other things, I actually felt that at the end of the day, when I was 35 or 6, when it was all over I'd done as much with my body and the talent that I had, that I could have done. I don't think that there's many players that can say that Bernie. I think a lot of them would say, if only I had worked harder, been a bit more professional, if only I hadn't got tied up with the wrong people, and I think I'm one of the few people that can say that I couldn't have done any better than I did.

BERNIE.

Recently you were voted Boro number one player of all time, how big an accolade was that?

GRAEME.

I believe that was from the players. Well that means everything, because ok supporters are not professionals and the things that they like in strikers, they might not see the good things in a defender, is that making sense? You might have a great goalkeeper, but because he's a great goalkeeper he makes things look simple. And I think for your fellow professionals, to say that about you then that's the ultimate isn't it.

BERNIE

I believe you had a good relationship with Willie Maddren, what were his qualities as a player, on and off the field?

GRAEME.

What was special about him on a professional side, we spoke earlier about what was a good professional. Willie was somebody who worked really hard at his game, he was the 1st one on the training pitch, I know its an old cliché 1st one on the training pitch last one to leave, but that was Willie, and even in the early days he had a dodgy knee, and you had to keep dragging him off the training ground, but that was Willie he always wanted to do that bit more.

He took that into the games of football he played, he always wanted to do a bit more help his team mates been the one that was always leading the way And err that's what made him a great player, apart from the natural ability that he had, he wanted to help other people and he had a natural gift for that, but he was a hell of a player, and again even from an early age he had this problem his knee wasn't right, wasn't 100%, and he still was the best player on the pitch 9 times out of 10 when we played in that season, and that made him a very special player.

And then on the other side of things he was a very special man, and we were, he was my pal we roomed together, he was my good pal at the club and its absolutely tragic what's happened to him.

BERNIE.

You left Boro for Liverpool, why did you leave Boro and did you leave on a sour note?

GRAEME.

Yes, unfortunately. One New Year Liverpool wanted me, Liverpool were the best team around, and you had a real chance of winning things. Err it was neither the money or that I was unhappy at Middlesbrough for any reason, the biggest concern I'd had leaving Middlesbrough, wasn't leaving Middlesbrough football club it was leaving my land lady Feebie Haig and the family I had lived with, and it was the big problem I had leaving Middlesbrough, and that was the question that kept coming back to me, as much as I want to go to Liverpool and be part of the most successful team in Europe, as they were at the time I was leaving a situation and environment were I was so happy, and that was the biggest decision I had to make out of all of it.

BERNIE.

What about your success?

GRAEME

Any major trophies, if you win a championship, that's a special occasion, if you win 3 European cups its what dreams are made of, its ironic because at the time you think European Cup we've won, great you know its not that bigger deal cause Liverpool has always done that.

Then you look at the hype that's gone with Manchester United this year doing it, the normality of the whole thing comes home. But at the time we didn't think like that, before at Liverpool at the time there was always that feeling that what they tried to instil into you, you're a good player, your in a good team, but your not as good as the team who was before you and you were forever trying to be better than what you were and err it was another way of hitting you on the head and keeping your feet on the ground.

BERNIE.

You have always had this champagne Charlie image, you know, how have you coped with that?

GRAEME.

Yes I think I like champagne, if somebody else is buying it, I like a glass of champagne I think my pals or anyone who knows me would not agree that, that's me you know, from where I started as a young lad, I was one of 3 boys and we lived in a prefab a council prefab, father had 2 jobs to give us what we wanted, a very basic beginning and although I like the nicer things in life, as we all do I'm certainly not a Billy Big , maybe when I was a bit younger, maybe I had an attitude then, but certainly when you mature, I like to think I'm a straight forward guy.

BERNIE.

I must ask you as a boy, my boyhood hero and idol was Kenny Dalglish, what was he like on and off the field?

GRAEME.

Kenny off the pitch a miserable bugger, I'm sure you've met Kenny. Kenny's a unique character, he's somebody who you have to get to know him, you know he's full of one liners and you think that's his banter he puts up for strangers, once you get past that he's a very different person and you know I wouldn't profess to know everything about him, but I stayed in the same bedroom, sounds terrible, for 7 years and we shared rooms for 7 years and I know a hell of a lot about him, and on the pitch he was just simply the best, Bernie there just wasn't anyone better. In midfield your heads down and your maybe trying to get the ball back and you would just look for his socks, give it too him if you saw his socks and give it to him, he would make something happen, and he'd make the rest of us look great players.

BERNIE.

Leaving Anfield you moved to Sampdoria how did you enjoy your time in Italy?

GRAEME.

Tremendous tremendous, err I was lucky to go to Sampdoria who were on the way up, they were a young team and I had been brought in to be the farther figure to all these young players and I had the likes of Gianluca Vialli, Mancini, Who's now at Lazio, they had a lot of young players who were 18 and 19 and I was 31 when I went there. So I signed for 3 years and the 1st season went really well, we won the Italian Cup which was the 1st trophy Sampdoria had ever won. Then err the 2nd season not so great I think we finished 5th or 6th and then at the end of the 2nd season the president called me in Mantovana his name was, and asked me did I want to stay for a 3rd year, and I said yes I'm happy to stay, I enjoy it here, I'd just like you to buy some more quality and give us a real chance for the championship, cause the young players were only getting better. Then err within 2 weeks of me having that meeting with him, well immediately after that meeting he decided to sell a guy called Mattioli, who he had brought in to play with me, but he had turned around after 6 games and said he couldn't play with me, he could only play in my position, so the president gets me in at the end of the 2nd year and says, so you are happy to stay, I say "yes" he says "ok" then he immediately sold Mattioli, to Inter Millan, and within 2 weeks I had to go back in and say, look I've had this chance to go back to manage one of the biggest teams in Britain, I'd love to go and he was fantastic about it.

BERNIE.

Next move was to go back to Glasgow Rangers, people describe Glasgow as living in a goldfish bowl, how did you find it?

GRAEME.

Well I'm from Edinburgh, so I used to do the hours Journey, I would drive through Glasgow big footballing city and it's a village when it comes to football, there's a rumour every day, you know, so and so has been sold, so and so has been bought, err someone's having an affair with another woman, someone's left their wife. There's something everyday, and its hard to handle, but that's the pressure if you want to work for a big big club. But I enjoyed it, it was all new to me, I was privileged to be given the opportunity to start managing at such a young age, at such a big club, and I made lots of mistakes, and I got lots of things right, and we had 5 years where we were very successful and we left the club in great nick.

BERNIE.

What about today's game? England, Scotland and Continental.

GRAEME.

Well, I think when I was playing there was a big difference, but I think that's all changed, I think footballs become very similar, I think maybe because of stronger refereeing . I think our football at one time was quite, more aggressive and more up and at them style, and I think because the refereeing has become stronger in our country, I think that has made it more stronger, similar to what's happening on the continent, players are allowed to express themselves much better now, without the threat of someone coming through from behind and err its hard. People will always ask that question, why should it be any different, you play the same size of pitch, the same weight of ball, same rules.

BERNIE.

Looking at your Scotland career 54 caps?

GRAEME.

Guiltily I should have had more, because when we were at Liverpool, we were openly quietly encouraged not to go to play in friendly internationals. Liverpool at the time were playing in European cup games, league cup games, which was an important trophy then, FA cup and obviously the league games, and err we were encouraged not to go and play in friendlies, and Alan Hansen and I would never go and Kenny wanted to go and play in every game he could, I think he has got over 100 caps, I should have played more but...

BERNIE.

At this minute you're out of football, what are your plans for the future?

GRAEME

In football you know, you never know what's round the corner, I want to work I've always loved football, I will always love football, you will be the same. If you have played the game it never goes away, and I think as long as I'm drawing my breath, I will always love football, and I think I will always be in the situation that I will want to work, and err although I'm not working at the moment, I will wait for the phone to ring and if not I will have a great garden in few years time.

BERNIE

Graeme thanks very much

GRAEME

It's a pleasure Bernie a pleasure.

HONOURS

GRAEME JAMES SOUNESS

PLAYING CAREER HISTORY

1970-1972	Tottenham Hotspur
1972	Montreal Olympique
1972-1978	Middlesbrough
1978	West Adelaide
1978-1984	Liverpool
1984-1986	Sampdoria
1986-1991	Rangers
1974-1986	Scotland

MANAGERIAL CAREER HISTORY

1986-1991	Rangers
1991-1994	Liverpool
1995-1996	Galatasaray
1996-1997	Southampton
1997	Torino
1997-1999	SL Benfica
2000-2004	Blackburn Rovers
2004-2006	Newcastle united.

PLAYING HONOURS (winners)

Tottenham Hotspur
1968	FA Youth Cup

Middlesbrough
1973-74	Football League Second Division

Liverpool
1977-78	European Cup
1978-79	League Championship

1979-80	Charity Shield
1979-80	League Championship
1980-81	Charity Shield
1980-81	League Cup
1980-81	European Cup
1981-82	League Cup
1981-82	League Championship
1982-83	Charity Shield
1982-83	League Cup
1982-83	League Championship
1983-84	League Cup
1983-84	League Championship
1983-84	European Cup

Sampdoria

1984-85	Coppa Italia

Rangers

1986-87	Scottish League Cup
1986-87	Scottish premier League
1987-88	Scottish league Cup

MANAGERIAL HONOURS (winners)

Rangers

1986-87	Scottish League Cup
1986-87	Scottish Premier League
1987-88	Scottish League Cup
1988-89	Scottish League Cup
1988-89	Scottish Premier League
1989-90	Scottish Premier League
1990-91	Scottish League Cup
1990-91	Scottish Premier League.

Liverpool
1991-92   FA Cup

Galatasary
1995-96   Turkish Cup
1996-97   Turkish Super Cup

Blackburn Rovers

2001-02   League Cup

CAPS   54 Full caps for Scotland

'People may talk about the team of 66. It wasn't, it was the squad of 66.'

Nobby on how England won the World Cup.

Take 15
Nobby Stiles

Norbert Stiles was born in Collyhurst, Manchester, on May 18th 1942.

After 14 years at the Theatre Of Dreams (Old Trafford), he was transferred to Middlesbrough in May 1971, for around £ 20,000.

Stan Anderson signed him and immediately made him captain, but unfortunately his appearances were restricted, due to injuries and loss of form.

I arranged to meet Nobby in a hotel in Newcastle.

I had obviously heard of Nobby and his fantastic achievements, but I had never met him.

He was smartly dressed, with Elton John sized glasses on.

I found him humorous, dry and humble when talking about his career.

BERNIE.

You started your career at old Trafford, as a Manchester lad you must have been delighted to wear the red shirt?

NOBBY

Oh yeh, dreamed of it when I was a kid.

Er my first memories are of listening to the1948 cup final ,at 6 years of age.

Then me brothers and me uncle used to take me down to Old Trafford ,when I was a kid.

And I used to dream when they announced the team that I'd be walking out there.

So to join Manchester Utd, obviously at 15 was great.

BERNIE

You were one of the England stars in the 1966 World Cup triumph. How did you do it ?

NOBBY

It was Alf Ramsay. Alf Ramsay didn't say we could win the World Cup, Alf Ramsay kept saying we would win the World Cup.

I think if you asked the players at the start, we could win it, there was a belief in ourselves.

But Alf Ramsay gave us this belief, that we would win it, and as we went along in the tournament, the amazing thing was people talked about the team of 66 . It wasn't it was the squad of 66, I mean the bond between the players, like Ian Callaghan, Ron Flowers, Ron Springett, tremendous, so if you kicked one of us you kicked all of us, and Alf gave us that.

BERNIE

The 1966 World Cup squad has been honoured with MBE's, because of their success, long overdue ?

NOBBY

I don't know if it's overdue or not.

I know all the lads are delighted for each other.

Er George Cohen Rang me up and showed me a picture in the Express, where there's all the old fellows in shorts, it was a great caricature, you know. So yeh we're all pleased for each other. And if it's overdue or not, I'm delighted and I know the other lads are for each other.

BERNIE

Many peoples abiding memory of you, is doing some sort of a highland jig, with the World Cup in your hands.

NOBBY

It wasn't the highland jig (laughs).

The nice thing is all these years later, every 4 years they show the World Cup. So every 4 years, they show this fellow, with no teeth ,you know, I was skipping

, I was so delighted, so proud, I was over the moon, you know. But they call it the jig, so every 4 years the grandkids now say who is that, and they say it's Nobby Stiles, so it's nice to remember.

BERNIE

What type of player where you ?

NOBBY

Er, as I said when I started off at Manchester Utd, I started off as an attacking winger, finished up playing alongside Bill Faulkes at the back.

For England I played in midfield, so basically my job as I say was to win the ball.

I was a tackler, also I could read the game.

Erm if you ever watched on some of the old England games, during the World Cup, and before or whatever, Bobby Moore could come out like anything. Bobby Moore would come out the back, Ray Wilson and George Cohen, were always bombing forward and I just automatically, if they bombed forward I just dropped back in. It was just a natural reaction, Alf Ramsay didn't say do that, and I think personally one of my best things, as I say was winning the ball, giving it early, but also reading the game.

BERNIE

You went on to win the European Cup, with Manchester United in 1968. How emotional was that?

NOBBY

Eh for me Bernie.

I remember George Best saying something, around the 70's, that he felt disappointed, he felt let down, that he felt that in 66 we had won it, but we should have gone on and won more. At the time I thought no I don't agree with you George, cause we got to the semi final, against A C Milan, had a good go and we lost 2-1 on aggregate.

But having said that I think he was right, cause in a way, I think us older players, we were a bit older than George, had said well we've done it and we've done it for Sir Matt and that's it.

Eh I remember being with Alex Ferguson , back at Old Trafford, after they had won the league for the very 1st time. And he got all the staff out before we started the training. He said ' I want you's to watch the 1st team training , I'm not worried about the other lads , you can train them later. I want you's to have a look in the player's eyes, and see if the desire is still there.'

And I thought that's tremendous. That's why I remembered George.

In a way we had let George down , cause I think we did that , we had done it for Sir Matt, that's it even though we came up against AC Milan. I don't think we had that "umph" we're going to nail them.

I think in a way we thought oh we can beat these. You can't do that.

BERNIE

You moved to Middlesbrough in 1971, what attracted you to Teesside ?

NOBBY.

Wilf Mannion (laughs).

No, I mean when I was a kid at Old Trafford , starting off at Old Trafford, every team that came always had a few stars, you know.

But I always remember Wilf Mannion .

Me father had kept telling me about this man.

This is the Golden Boy with the blonde hair, and I saw Wilf Mannion, and I saw this small man .

I thought what a great player.

So when it was time for me to move, Harold Shepherdson had a word with me and whatever, and I just wanted to meet Wilf Mannion.

I never met him when I joined, but I met him years and years later, down in Eston when I was speaking there a few years ago. And he came up to me and I said 'Wilf it's a pleasure to meet you, and I've been dying to meet you all these years.' And he said 'Yeh' he said ' you went to St Patrick's, didn't you?' I said ' how did you know that?' ' well I went to St Peters.'

I thought well he's been looking out for me as well . Which was lovely.

BERNIE

In your 1st season at Middlesbrough, you went on a great F A Cup run, in fact it was FA Cup 5th round, you appeared at Old Trafford . What kind of reception did you receive?

NOBBY

Terrific, terrific.

BERNIE

Did you expect that?

NOBBY

No , I didn't actually, you know . I mean I was a United lad, and supported United, so going back there, err, I thought well, I was playing for Middlesbrough, I wanted Middlesbrough to win and it was a great result.

I thought we could have won the 1st game there and I wanted to do it.

But the reception I got, when I came out was terrific .And as I say we got a draw. And the sad thing was, when we came back, I think if it was a night match, the atmosphere was a bit different, I think we could have done it.

As it was they beat us well in the afternoon, because it was the time of the electricity cuts or whatever. And they beat us 3-0, and they beat us well, you know.

BERNIE

You were talking earlier, about underachieving . Do you think yourself and the team underachieved ?

NOBBY

Err I cant say for the other lads, I cant say for the other lads. I would never put that on them.

Err as I say, for myself, er I underachieved for Middlesbrough, yeh and as I say my knee wasn't the same, I wasn't the same, I was hoping I would be, I was hoping, I had ambitions that I could get back in the England team, cause my time was up at Old Trafford, I knew that, I had been there 14 years, and when the time comes ,you got to go.

But as I say, I found it disappointing that I didn't do well for Middlesbrough, but

I never regretted the move, and as I say I met a lot of good friends.

And er maybe it was the red as well, moving up to play in red.

BERNIE

Manager Stan Anderson left Big Jack took over, surprisingly you didn't feature in his plans.

Did you get on with Big Jack ?

NOBBY

Yeh, yeh, Jack was great, Jack was terrific and he was right.

Er you've got to go on, an he's got to make his decisions. But I was happy to move anyway.

Er to get back to Manchester, for the kids or whatever, and a lot of our old friends down there.

No I didn't regret it at all.

The only thing that bothered me was, I had moved to Yarm and I was down in Manchester, right in the inner city, and I lived in Stretford and Yarm, and what used to drive me mad was the birds singing and the cows mooing , it was doing me head in.(laughs)

I was a Manchester lad, I'd have been better staying in Linthorpe.

Anyway I moved to Yarm, though it was beautiful, the birds were waking me up with their singing.

But as I say , I met a lot of good friends, and they still are.

I never regretted the move.

BERNIE

People associate you with the like of Manchester United and England, but do you still have a soft spot for Middlesbrough ?

NOBBY

Oh yeh, yeh .As I said the big thing is I always look out for Middlesbrough.

I always look out for Boro's results or whatever.

And I was delighted when Big Jack did what he did.

Er I was delighted at them coming back up, I hope Robbo keeps them up, and I wish them well.

No doubt about it because as I said my big thing was Wilf Mannion, and Wilf Mannion is always going to be there, for me and for Middlesbrough.

I thought he was one of the greatest players I ever saw.

So just to be just a part of it ,is something special.

HONOURS

NORBERT PETER STILES

PLAYING CAREER HISTORY

1960-1971	Manchester United
1971-1973	Middlesbrough
1973-1975	Preston North End
1965-1970	England

MANAGERIAL CAREER HISTORY

1977-1981	Preston North End
1981-1984	Vancouver Whitecaps
1985-1986	West Bromwich

PLAYING HONOURS (winners)

England

1966	World Cup

Manchester United

1963	FA Cup
1964-1965	League Championship
1965	FA Charity Shield
1966-1967	European Cup
1967-1968	European Cup
1967	FA Charity Shield

CAPS	28 Full caps for England

This pic is myself with the late great Wilf Mannion taken at the "Ladle Hotel" in Marton

Me with Big Jack at his home in Newcastle

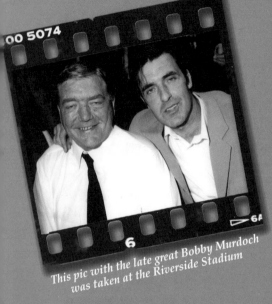

This pic with the late great Bobby Murdoch was taken at the Riverside Stadium

Pic taken with Juninho at a book signing session at the club shop in Captain Cook Square

Pic taken in Nottingham at Brian Clough's friend's house

I met up with Chris "yet again" at the Premier League Allstars in London at the 02